Eyewitness
ARMS &
ARMOR

Silver-hilted
robe sword,
c. 1710

Flintlock pocket
pistol, c. 1770

Rapier, c. 1625

Silver-hilted
hunting sword,
c. 1750

Flintlock
"Tower" pistol,
c. 1800

Pepperbox revolver,
c. 1855

Medieval dagger, c. 1400

Gauntlet, c. 1580

Pinfire revolver,
c. 1860

Cartridges,
c. 1850

Eyewitness
ARMS &
ARMOR

Written by
MICHELE BYAM

Indian knife
with jade hilt,
c. 1800

Howdah pistol,
c. 1850

Powder flask, c. 1850

Belgian crossbow,
c. 1830

Three
Indian arrows,
c. 1800

German war hammer, c. 1600

DK
DK Publishing, Inc.

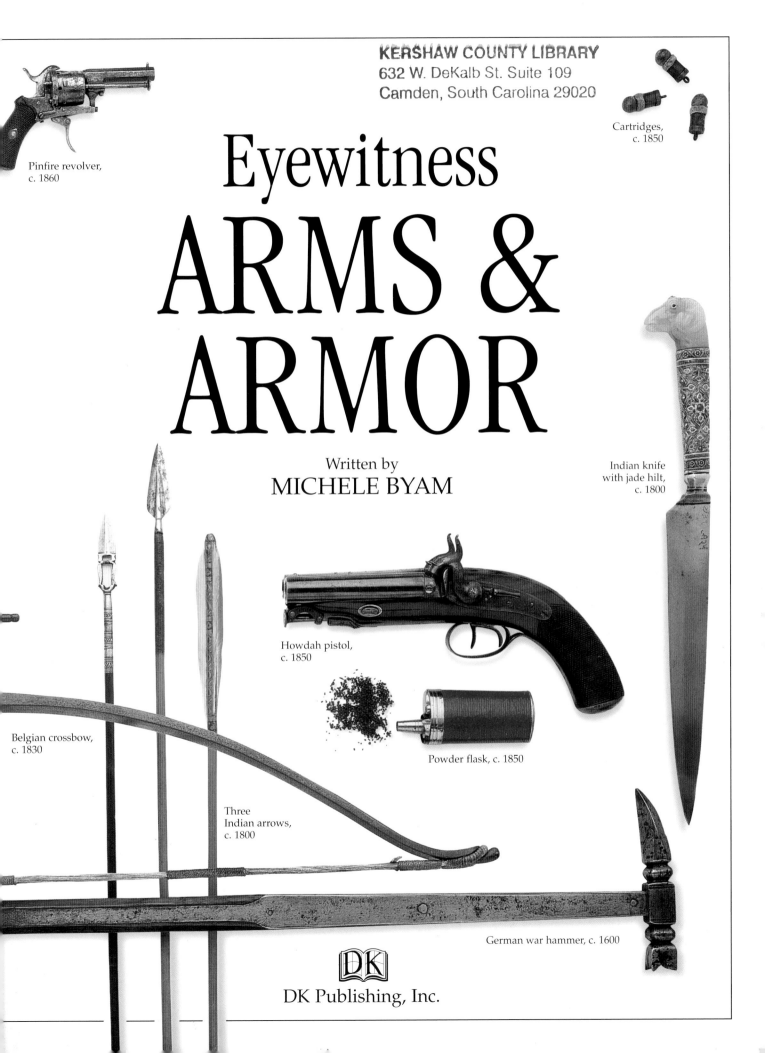

LONDON, NEW YORK, MELBOURNE,
MUNICH, and DELHI

Maratha "crow-bill" war
pick from northern India

Niam Niam, a ceremonial
knife from Sudan

Project editor Michèle Byam
Managing art editor Jane Owen
Special photography Dave King
Editorial consultant David Harding

REVISED EDITION
Managing editor Andrew Macintyre
Managing art editor Jane Thomas
Category publisher Linda Martin
Art director Simon Webb
Editor and reference compiler Sue Nicholson
Art editor Andrew Nash
Production Jenny Jacoby
Picture research Sarah Pownall
DTP Designer Siu Yin Ho

U.S. editor Elizabeth Hester
Senior editor Beth Sutinis
Art director Dirk Kaufman
U.S. DTP designer Milos Orlovic
U.S. production Chris Avgherinos

This Eyewitness ® Guide has been conceived by
Dorling Kindersley Limited and Editions Gallimard

This edition published in the United States in 2004
by DK Publishing, Inc.
375 Hudson Street, New York, NY 10014

04 05 06 07 08 10 9 8 7 6 5 4 3 2 1

Copyright © 1988, © 2004, Dorling Kindersley Limited

A catalog record for this book is available from the Library of Congress.

ISBN 0-7566-0654-3 (HC) 0-7566-0653-5 (Library Binding)

Color reproduction by Colourscan, Singapore
Printed in China by Toppan Printing Co.,
(Shenzhen) Ltd.

Copper dagger of the
Kasai people in
West Africa

Discover more at

www.dk.com

Chinese sword in
wooden sheath
clad in tortoiseshell
with brass mounts

Contents

Spiked iron
bracelet
from eastern
Sudan

Buffalo horn
knuckleduster
from southern India

Prehistoric weapons

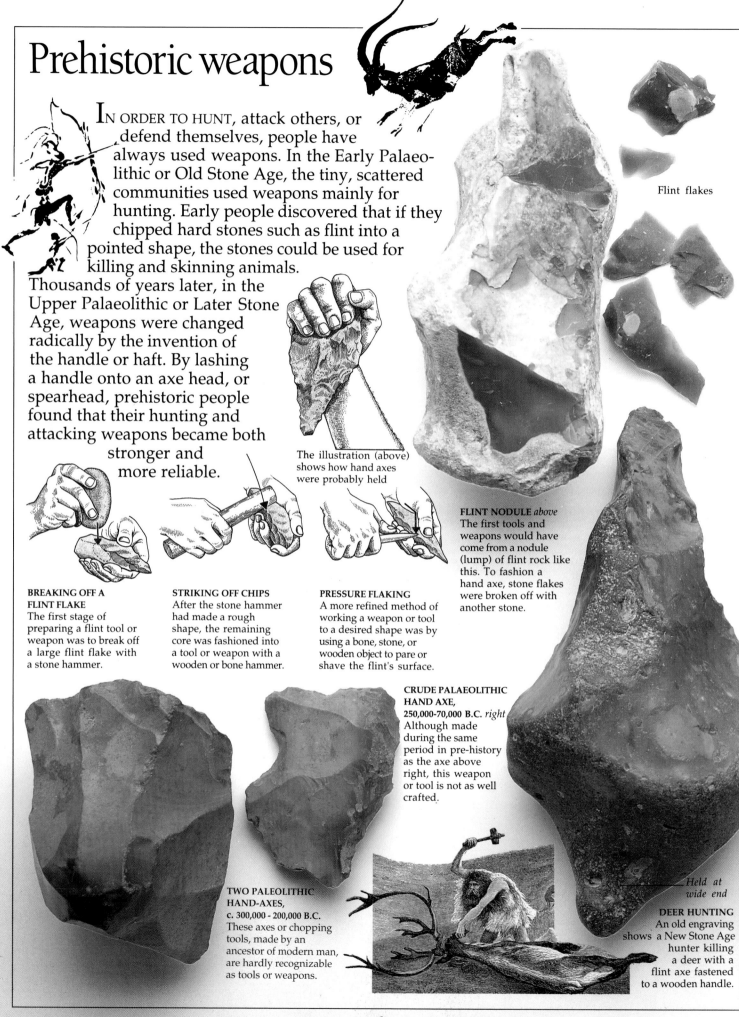

IN ORDER TO HUNT, attack others, or defend themselves, people have always used weapons. In the Early Palaeolithic or Old Stone Age, the tiny, scattered communities used weapons mainly for hunting. Early people discovered that if they chipped hard stones such as flint into a pointed shape, the stones could be used for killing and skinning animals.

Thousands of years later, in the Upper Palaeolithic or Later Stone Age, weapons were changed radically by the invention of the handle or haft. By lashing a handle onto an axe head, or spearhead, prehistoric people found that their hunting and attacking weapons became both stronger and more reliable.

Flint flakes

The illustration (above) shows how hand axes were probably held

BREAKING OFF A FLINT FLAKE
The first stage of preparing a flint tool or weapon was to break off a large flint flake with a stone hammer.

STRIKING OFF CHIPS
After the stone hammer had made a rough shape, the remaining core was fashioned into a tool or weapon with a wooden or bone hammer.

PRESSURE FLAKING
A more refined method of working a weapon or tool to a desired shape was by using a bone, stone, or wooden object to pare or shave the flint's surface.

FLINT NODULE *above*
The first tools and weapons would have come from a nodule (lump) of flint rock like this. To fashion a hand axe, stone flakes were broken off with another stone.

CRUDE PALAEOLITHIC HAND AXE,
250,000-70,000 B.C. *right*
Although made during the same period in pre-history as the axe above right, this weapon or tool is not as well crafted.

TWO PALEOLITHIC HAND-AXES,
c. 300,000 - 200,000 B.C.
These axes or chopping tools, made by an ancestor of modern man, are hardly recognizable as tools or weapons.

Held at wide end

DEER HUNTING
An old engraving shows a New Stone Age hunter killing a deer with a flint axe fastened to a wooden handle.

6

TWO SHAPED PALAEOLITHIC HAND AXES,
c. 250,000-70,000 B.C. *left and below*
Hand axes were certainly used by
Palaeolithic people as weapons
when hunting animals, but it is
purely guesswork whether an axe
like this was ever used as a
battle-axe in warfare.

Rough cutting edge

**MIDDLE PALAEOLITHIC
HAND AXES,**
c. 80,000-40,000 B.C. *right*
Of a similar date, these
two hand axes were
made by a type of early
people known as
Neanderthal man.

A cave painting of archers,
painted between 12,000 and 3,000
B.C., found at Cueva Remigia,
Spain (above)

Spearhead tip

SPEARHEAD, c. 20,000 B.C.
By the time this possible
spearhead was made by
Homo sapiens sapiens or
modern man, handles
had been invented,
which radically
changed weapons
and tools.

A STONE AGE MAMMOTH HUNT
Hunters in the Old Stone Age needed both bravery
and cleverness to trap and kill large animals. Having
been driven into a pit, this woolly mammoth, an
extinct type of elephant, is being battered to
death with rocks. The spears sticking into the
mammoth's sides would have been
made of sharpened wood.

**STONE AGE
HUNTERS**
Cave paintings
found in European
countries such as
Spain and France
show either hunters
or the animals
they killed.

Missile weapons

ANYONE WHO HAS EVER thrown a stick or a stone, fired a catapult, or shot an arrow from a bow has used a missile weapon. Indeed, such weapons have been used for both hunting and fighting since prehistoric times. More unusual missile weapons include the boomerang, traditional weapon of the native Australian aborigine, and the curiously shaped throwing weapons used by the tribespeople of Central and West Africa. The simplicity of these weapons is deceptive, for when used by skilled throwers they are just as effective as more complex hand weapons.

Stone arrowhead

ASSYRIAN HORSEMAN
In this 7th century B.C. relief, an Assyrian carries a lance, a sword, and a bow with arrows.

Flatter on one side than the other

FIGHTING BOOMERANG *left*
The large wooden boomerangs used by aborigines in war are designed to fly straight and do not return to their throwers even if they miss their targets.

Flat piece of hard wood

Grip

Striking edge

THROWING A BOOMERANG
When used by a skilled thrower, such as this Australian aborigine, a boomerang can be sent great distances.

PARRYING STICK *above*
Sticks are defensive rather than offensive weapons. This aborigine parrying stick deflects missile weapons such as spears and boomerangs.

Club's pointed end

THROWING CLUB *above right*
An aborigine aiming this wooden throwing club would try to stun his victim with the weapon's pointed end. Some of the wooden war clubs used by Pacific Islanders and African tribesmen are also used as missile weapons.

ABORIGINES HUNTING
Australian aborigines are peaceful people who rarely use their weapons for fighting. In this 19th-century painting a group of aborigines are hunting game with hand clubs, shields, and multi-tipped fishing spears.

ABORIGINAL SPEAR *above*
Made of stone or bone, the heads of Aboriginal throwing-spears are made in much the same way as spears used by Stone Age hunters (p. 7).

Protective arrow sheath

Poisoned tip

SHORT BOW
Although bows are popular all over the world, only a few tribespeople make poisoned arrows. This bow and poisoned arrow come from West Africa.

Assyrian archer shooting a short bow

King from ancient Persia (Iran) using a bow and arrow

Striking edge

THROWING AXES
Although steel throwing axes were popular in Europe only during the Middle Ages, they have always been used by certain African tribes. Both these throwing axes were made in West Africa, c. 1900.

THROWING KNIFE
Among the most unusual-looking weapons are African throwing knives. A multi-bladed weapon always has a better than average chance of striking its target.

Short handle

THE STAFF SLING *below*
Slings were used by European armies for hurling rocks until the 16th century. The staff sling, a shaft with a leather sling fixed to one end, could hurl stones with tremendous force.

An Anglo-Saxon slinger releasing his sling (left)

Holding a sling (above)

The first warriors

THE DISCOVERY OF METALS such as copper, bronze, and iron revolutionized the making of tools and weapons, since each was progressively harder and stronger. Bronze, made by mixing metals, was first used in southwest Europe about six thousand years ago. In the early part of the Bronze Age, axes and spears were still tanged (bound to a handle or haft by leather strips or string), but by the end of the Bronze Age, weapons were more firmly secured to handles by sockets. In the 6th and 7th century B.C., Celtic tribesmen began to make iron as well as bronze tools and weapons, and their richly ornamental culture is well-illustrated by these finely crafted artifacts.

A fragment of copper or bronze, used for making weapons or tools

Socket for insertion of haft (handle)

Three flint arrowheads

Tang

Barb

Loop through which a cord tied axehead to haft

HALBERD BLADE,
c. 2300-1600 B.C. *below*
Made either in Ireland or on the European mainland, this copper halberd could be used for either cutting or chopping, thus combining the uses of a battle-ax and spear.

FLINT ARROWHEADS,
c. 2700-1800 B.C. *above*
Bows and arrows were used for the first time during the Mesolithic Age (Middle Stone Age). About 2500 B.C. these "barbed and tanged" arrowheads were used for hunting or warfare.

Celtic warrior, c. 450 B.C., carrying a sword and spear

BRONZE SPEARHEAD,
c. 900-800 B.C. *above*
Crude spears were first used in the New Stone Age (pp. 6-7). By the Bronze Age, spearheads like this were made by skilled bronzesmiths.

THREE BRONZE AXE HEADS,
c. 750-650 B.C.
By the Late European Bronze Age, bronzesmiths had learned to make socketed axes into which wooden handles were inserted. Axes were used for warfare or woodworking.

BRONZE SWORD POMMELS AND HILTS
The fine engraving on these swords shows the craftsmanship of Late Bronze Age bronzesmiths. Weapons like these would have belonged to chieftains.

Grip would have had wood, bone, or horn plates, riveted on either side and wrapped with leather

BRONZE AGE SWORD, c. 900-800 B.C.
This gracefully shaped Late Bronze Age sword was designed as a slashing weapon.

Double-edged blade

Long wooden handle

10

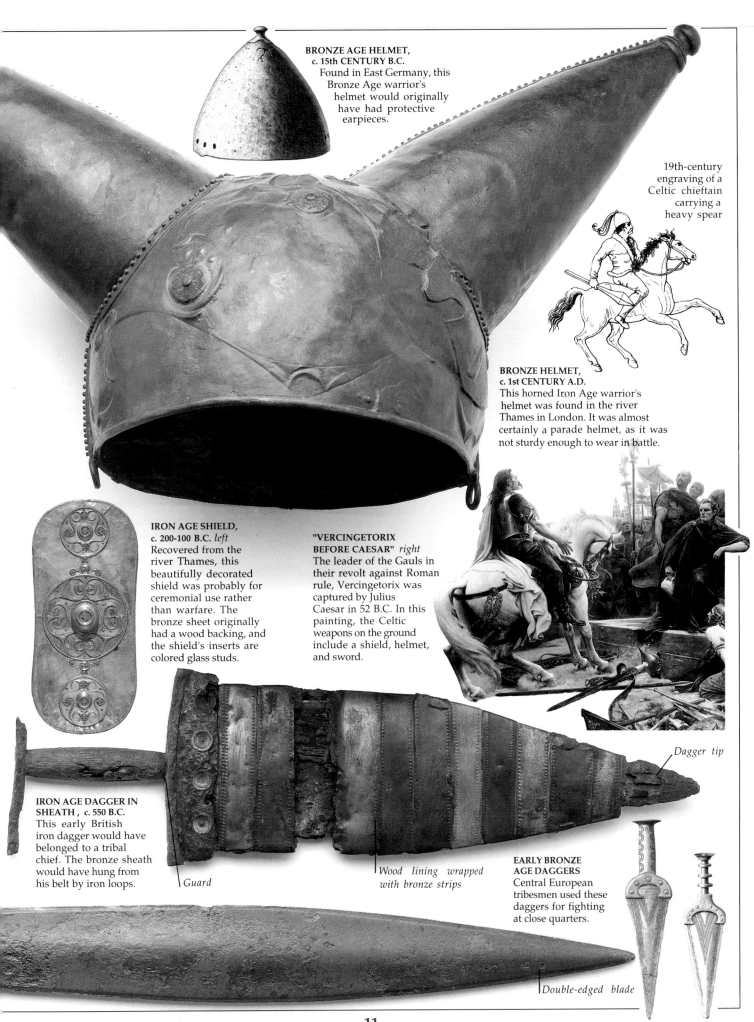

BRONZE AGE HELMET,
c. 15th CENTURY B.C.
Found in East Germany, this
Bronze Age warrior's
helmet would originally
have had protective
earpieces.

19th-century
engraving of a
Celtic chieftain
carrying a
heavy spear

BRONZE HELMET,
c. 1st CENTURY A.D.
This horned Iron Age warrior's
helmet was found in the river
Thames in London. It was almost
certainly a parade helmet, as it was
not sturdy enough to wear in battle.

IRON AGE SHIELD,
c. 200-100 B.C. *left*
Recovered from the
river Thames, this
beautifully decorated
shield was probably for
ceremonial use rather
than warfare. The
bronze sheet originally
had a wood backing, and
the shield's inserts are
colored glass studs.

"VERCINGETORIX
BEFORE CAESAR" *right*
The leader of the Gauls in
their revolt against Roman
rule, Vercingetorix was
captured by Julius
Caesar in 52 B.C. In this
painting, the Celtic
weapons on the ground
include a shield, helmet,
and sword.

Dagger tip

IRON AGE DAGGER IN
SHEATH , c. 550 B.C.
This early British
iron dagger would have
belonged to a tribal
chief. The bronze sheath
would have hung from
his belt by iron loops.

Wood lining wrapped
with bronze strips

EARLY BRONZE
AGE DAGGERS
Central European
tribesmen used these
daggers for fighting
at close quarters.

Guard

Double-edged blade

Greeks and Romans

THE TWO GREATEST ARMIES of ancient times were the Macedonian army under Alexander the Great and the Roman army. From 334 to 326 B.C., Macedonia, a small Greek state, had a superb army built around the phalanx – solid lines of spear-carrying infantry. The basis of the Roman army was the legion – units of infantry with supporting cavalry. Between 800 B.C. and A.D. 200, it was the Roman army's continuing responses to enemy weapons and to the changes in available materials, coupled with good discipline and an efficient organizational ability, that brought Rome to its preeminent position as ruler of the ancient world. The Roman armor and weapons shown on these pages are accurate replicas of equipment carried by the legions.

A Roman standard-bearer wearing a *gladius*

A Greek hoplite

A Greek foot soldier or hoplite's armor included a metal helmet, a breastplate made of bronze or layers of linen reinforced by scales or plates, a metal shield, and leg armor.

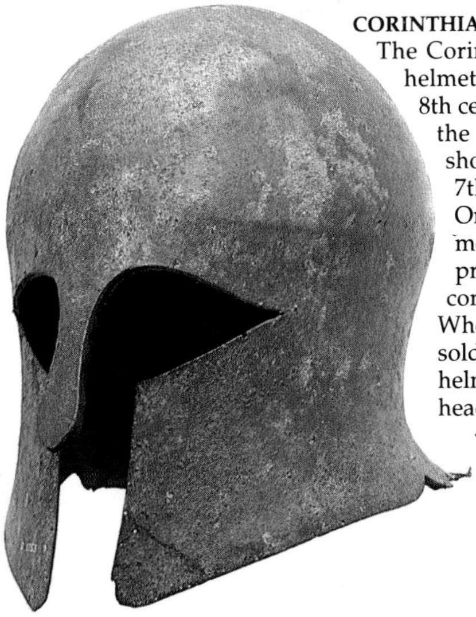

Gladius *handle made of wood or bone*

MILITARY DAGGER
Soldiers carried a short dagger called a *pugio* on the belt at their left hip. Its iron scabbard was often decorated with inlaid enamel patterns. Roman works of art only depict soldiers wearing a *pugio* in the lst centuries B.C. to A.D., which suggests that it was not considered an essential weapon.

Grip made of bronze

INFANTRY SWORD
The *gladius* was a short, double-edged sword that was used more for thrusting than for cutting. It was worn by infantrymen at the right hip either on a belt or a baldric (shoulder belt). The scabbard was sometimes highly decorated, as in this example from the 1st century A.D.

Double-edged blade

CORINTHIAN HELMET
The Corinthian-type Greek helmet, first made in the 8th century B.C., reached the elegant shape shown here in the 7th century B.C. Only the eyes and mouth were uncovered, providing almost complete protection. When not fighting, the soldier often wore his helmet on top of his head for comfort.

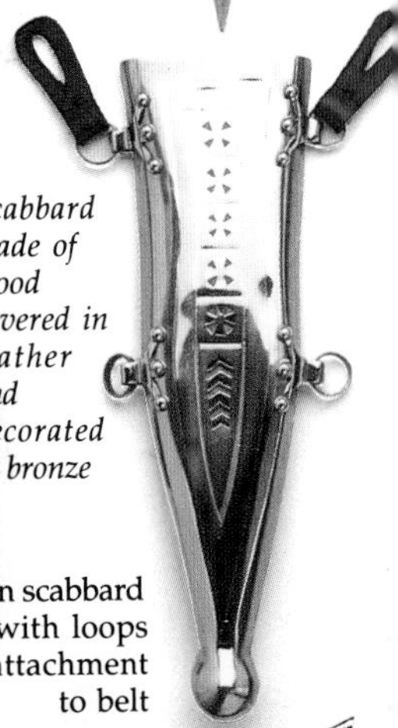

Scabbard made of wood covered in leather and decorated in bronze

Iron scabbard with loops for attachment to belt

SCENE FROM THE ILIAD
A Victorian depiction of soliders from the Greek epic poem the *Iliad*. Written in the 8th century B.C. and attributed to Homer, the poem tells of the events in the final year of the mythological Trojan War. The warrior on the left is wearing his sword on his right hip, Roman-style.

SCENE FROM THE ILIAD
A 19th-century picture of soldiers from the Greek epic poem the *Iliad*. Said to have been written in the 8th century B.C. by Homer, the poem tells of events in the final year of the mythological Trojan War. The warriors are in fact wearing Roman-style bronze breastplates and helmets.

Long iron point

Horsehair crest

Holder for horsehair crest

IRON HELMET
The iron Imperial Gallic helmet (c. A.D. 50 to 150) had a deep neck guard, a brow guard to deflect sword strokes, and cheekpieces of doubtful value.

BRONZE HELMET
This bronze helmet (c.50 B.C.) is a very simple design that carried a horsehair crest. Later helmets of this type had feathered crests.

Broad cheekpieces hinged to side of helmet and tied under chin with straps or cords

THROWING SPEARS *left*
The head of the *hasta* (right) is a familiar shape for a spear, but the long head of the *pilum* (left) was designed to pierce a shield and then continue on into the soldier behind it.

ROMAN GLADIATORS
Although their style was more flamboyant than that of the Roman army, gladiators had similar weapons and armor, such as swords and rectangular shields.

Armor laced together at the front and upper part of armor hooked to lower part by bronze hooks

BODY ARMOR
Made of iron strips, the *lorica segmentata*, an early cuirass (p. 26), was worn from early in the 1st century A.D. until the 3rd century. It partially replaced the earlier chain mail and scale armor. The strips were held together by leather straps on the inside, and the armor had many bronze fittings.

Victorian depiction of Roman legionaries

Long haft made of ash

Weapons from Barbarian Europe

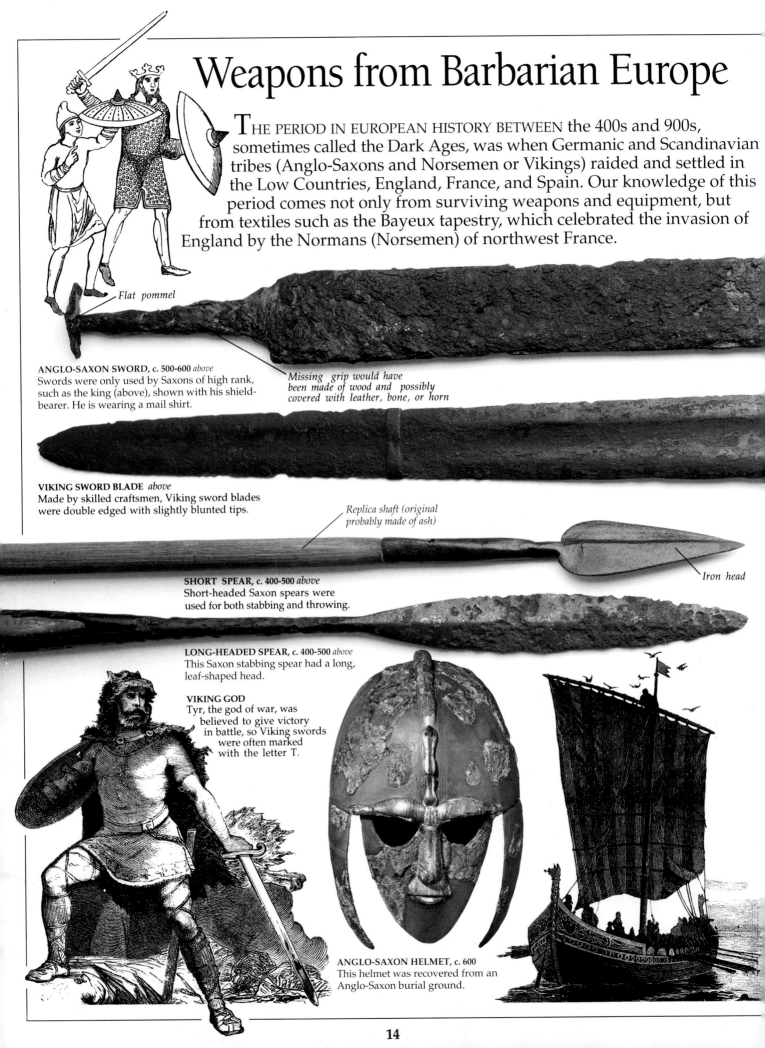

THE PERIOD IN EUROPEAN HISTORY BETWEEN the 400s and 900s, sometimes called the Dark Ages, was when Germanic and Scandinavian tribes (Anglo-Saxons and Norsemen or Vikings) raided and settled in the Low Countries, England, France, and Spain. Our knowledge of this period comes not only from surviving weapons and equipment, but from textiles such as the Bayeux tapestry, which celebrated the invasion of England by the Normans (Norsemen) of northwest France.

Flat pommel

ANGLO-SAXON SWORD, c. 500-600 *above*
Swords were only used by Saxons of high rank, such as the king (above), shown with his shield-bearer. He is wearing a mail shirt.

Missing grip would have been made of wood and possibly covered with leather, bone, or horn

VIKING SWORD BLADE *above*
Made by skilled craftsmen, Viking sword blades were double edged with slightly blunted tips.

Replica shaft (original probably made of ash)

SHORT SPEAR, c. 400-500 *above*
Short-headed Saxon spears were used for both stabbing and throwing.

Iron head

LONG-HEADED SPEAR, c. 400-500 *above*
This Saxon stabbing spear had a long, leaf-shaped head.

VIKING GOD
Tyr, the god of war, was believed to give victory in battle, so Viking swords were often marked with the letter T.

ANGLO-SAXON HELMET, c. 600
This helmet was recovered from an Anglo-Saxon burial ground.

THE NORMANS ATTACK THE ENGLISH

A valuable document on the weapons of the Norman period, the Bayeux tapestry is a strip of embroidered linen that chronicles the Norman invasion of England in 1066.

Inlaid pattern

SWORD GUARD, c. 1040
Made of metal, ivory, bone or horn, sword guards were often inlaid with precious metals.

Rounded point

Shallow fuller (groove) lightens weight of blade

Curved cross-guard

Trilobed pommel

VIKING SWORD, c. 900-1000 *below*
A Viking's favorite weapon was his sword. Used for slashing rather than thrusting at an enemy, swords were carried in decorated scabbards.

Grips, made of metal, horn, wood, or bone, were sometimes covered in leather

VIKING AXE, c. 900-1000
A Viking warrior swung his battle-axe around his head in an arc before landing an almost certainly fatal blow on an enemy or his horse.

NORMAN ARCHER *right*
This detail from the Bayeux tapestry (above) shows an archer with a quiver full of arrows. He is the only archer depicted on the tapestry wearing a mail shirt.

Norman knights using spurs and stirrups

NORMAN SPUR, c. 11th CENTURY
First used in ancient Greece and Rome, spurs helped the Norman knight, a skillful horseman, to control his horse in battle.

Long handle for holding with two hands

Broad, crescent-shaped blade

Cutting edge made of hardened steel

Three Norman arrows (above and below)

Arrowhead made of iron

THE DISCOVERY OF GREENLAND
Explorers as well as warriors and traders, the Vikings, led by Eric the Red, discovered and colonized Greenland in c. 982.

Sharply pointed Norman lance

European swords

ONE OF HUMANITY'S OLDEST WEAPONS, a sword consists of a hilt and a blade: the hilt has a pommel for balancing the weapon, a grip for holding it, and a guard for protecting the hand. The blade can be straight or curved and, according to whether the sword is designed for cutting, thrusting, or both, is either single or double edged, and has a rounded or pointed tip. For centuries, swords were used mainly for cutting and were held with one hand. But by the 1400s, larger swords came into use that were wielded with two hands, such as the Scottish claymore.

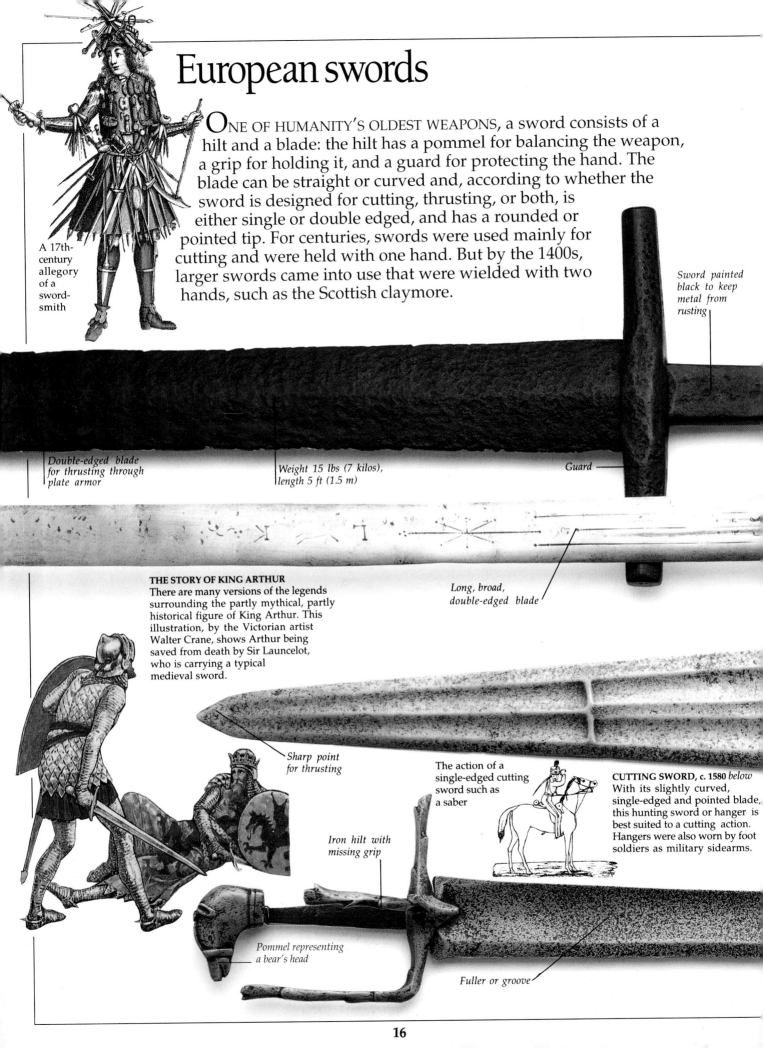

Sword painted black to keep metal from rusting

Double-edged blade for thrusting through plate armor

Weight 15 lbs (7 kilos), length 5 ft (1.5 m)

Guard

Long, broad, double-edged blade

THE STORY OF KING ARTHUR
There are many versions of the legends surrounding the partly mythical, partly historical figure of King Arthur. This illustration, by the Victorian artist Walter Crane, shows Arthur being saved from death by Sir Launcelot, who is carrying a typical medieval sword.

Sharp point for thrusting

The action of a single-edged cutting sword such as a saber

Iron hilt with missing grip

CUTTING SWORD, c. 1580 *below*
With its slightly curved, single-edged and pointed blade, this hunting sword or hanger is best suited to a cutting action. Hangers were also worn by foot soldiers as military sidearms.

Pommel representing a bear's head

Fuller or groove

16

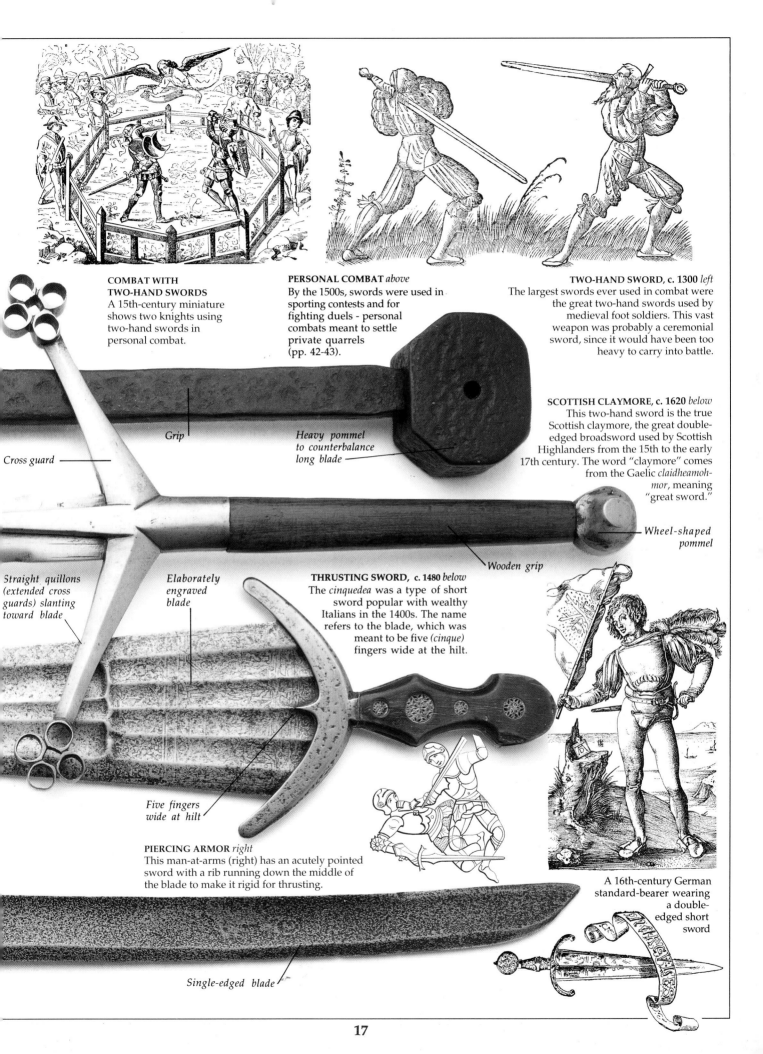

COMBAT WITH TWO-HAND SWORDS
A 15th-century miniature shows two knights using two-hand swords in personal combat.

PERSONAL COMBAT *above*
By the 1500s, swords were used in sporting contests and for fighting duels - personal combats meant to settle private quarrels (pp. 42-43).

TWO-HAND SWORD, c. 1300 *left*
The largest swords ever used in combat were the great two-hand swords used by medieval foot soldiers. This vast weapon was probably a ceremonial sword, since it would have been too heavy to carry into battle.

Grip

Heavy pommel to counterbalance long blade

Cross guard

SCOTTISH CLAYMORE, c. 1620 *below*
This two-hand sword is the true Scottish claymore, the great double-edged broadsword used by Scottish Highlanders from the 15th to the early 17th century. The word "claymore" comes from the Gaelic *claidheamoh-mor*, meaning "great sword."

Wheel-shaped pommel

Straight quillons (extended cross guards) slanting toward blade

Elaborately engraved blade

Wooden grip

THRUSTING SWORD, c. 1480 *below*
The *cinquedea* was a type of short sword popular with wealthy Italians in the 1400s. The name refers to the blade, which was meant to be five *(cinque)* fingers wide at the hilt.

Five fingers wide at hilt

PIERCING ARMOR *right*
This man-at-arms (right) has an acutely pointed sword with a rib running down the middle of the blade to make it rigid for thrusting.

Single-edged blade

A 16th-century German standard-bearer wearing a double-edged short sword

Crossbow and longbow

DURING THE MIDDLE AGES the use of the bow in both hunting and battle was revolutionized by the appearance of the longbow and the crossbow. By combining archery with simple machinery, the crossbow often proved a more deadly weapon than the ordinary bow (p. 9). Indeed, some crossbows were so powerfully made that they had to be loaded by a variety of mechanical devices. But despite the crossbow's greater range, it had a slower rate of fire than the longbow and was more expensive to make. The longbow was a much improved version of the ordinary bow, and at a range of 300 ft (90 m), its steel-tipped arrows were deadly. With neither weapon having a clear lead over the other, many medieval armies had both longbowmen and crossbowmen.

Medieval iron arrowheads

Longbowmen, from a 15th-century manuscript

SOLDIER USING WINDLASS
Crossbows had a slow rate of fire because they had to be wound to pull back the bowstring before they could be shot. They were more useful, therefore, in sieges, where the rate of fire was less important.

Firing a crossbow

1 Bowstring held in spanned (loaded) position by a rotating catch (the nut) set in crossbow tiller.
2 Bolt laid in groove along the top of stock and aimed by pressing rear of stock to cheek.
3 Bolt then released by pressing up the rear end of the trigger.

ARCHERS DEFENDING A CITY *left*
During the 15th century many fortified towns trained archers to defend the city to which they belonged. Note the crossbowman winding a cranequin (see above).

Steel arrowhead missing from this arrow

ENGLISH LONGBOW, c. 19th century

ENGLISH YEW LONGBOW
Constructed from a single piece of wood, usually yew, the longbow was a formidable weapon when shot by highly trained archers. Longbow lengths varied from country to country, but in England the bow was usually the breadth of an archer's span between his outstretched arms, which in a tall man would equal his height.

Horn nock or groove for attaching bowstring

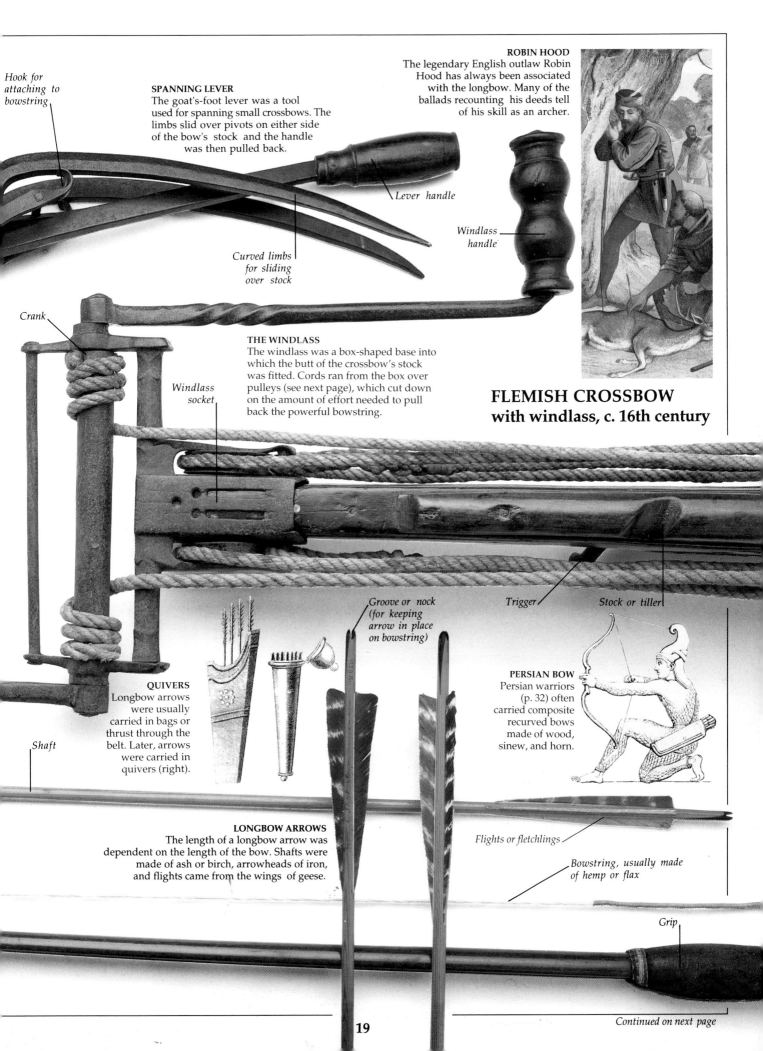

Hook for attaching to bowstring

SPANNING LEVER
The goat's-foot lever was a tool used for spanning small crossbows. The limbs slid over pivots on either side of the bow's stock and the handle was then pulled back.

Lever handle

Curved limbs for sliding over stock

ROBIN HOOD
The legendary English outlaw Robin Hood has always been associated with the longbow. Many of the ballads recounting his deeds tell of his skill as an archer.

Windlass handle

Crank

THE WINDLASS
The windlass was a box-shaped base into which the butt of the crossbow's stock was fitted. Cords ran from the box over pulleys (see next page), which cut down on the amount of effort needed to pull back the powerful bowstring.

Windlass socket

FLEMISH CROSSBOW
with windlass, c. 16th century

Groove or nock (for keeping arrow in place on bowstring)

Trigger

Stock or tiller

QUIVERS
Longbow arrows were usually carried in bags or thrust through the belt. Later, arrows were carried in quivers (right).

PERSIAN BOW
Persian warriors (p. 32) often carried composite recurved bows made of wood, sinew, and horn.

Shaft

LONGBOW ARROWS
The length of a longbow arrow was dependent on the length of the bow. Shafts were made of ash or birch, arrowheads of iron, and flights came from the wings of geese.

Flights or fletchlings

Bowstring, usually made of hemp or flax

Grip

Continued on next page

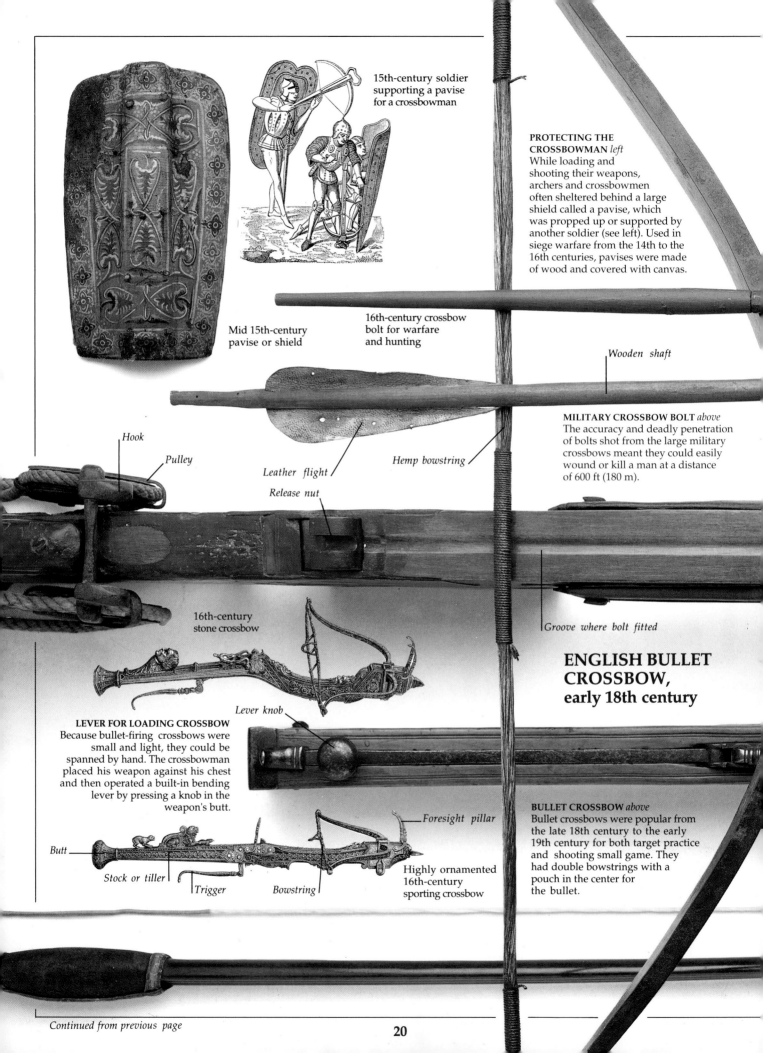

15th-century soldier supporting a pavise for a crossbowman

PROTECTING THE CROSSBOWMAN *left*
While loading and shooting their weapons, archers and crossbowmen often sheltered behind a large shield called a pavise, which was propped up or supported by another soldier (see left). Used in siege warfare from the 14th to the 16th centuries, pavises were made of wood and covered with canvas.

Mid 15th-century pavise or shield

16th-century crossbow bolt for warfare and hunting

Wooden shaft

MILITARY CROSSBOW BOLT *above*
The accuracy and deadly penetration of bolts shot from the large military crossbows meant they could easily wound or kill a man at a distance of 600 ft (180 m).

Hook

Pulley

Leather flight

Release nut

Hemp bowstring

Groove where bolt fitted

ENGLISH BULLET CROSSBOW, early 18th century

16th-century stone crossbow

Lever knob

LEVER FOR LOADING CROSSBOW
Because bullet-firing crossbows were small and light, they could be spanned by hand. The crossbowman placed his weapon against his chest and then operated a built-in bending lever by pressing a knob in the weapon's butt.

Foresight pillar

Butt

Stock or tiller

Trigger

Bowstring

Highly ornamented 16th-century sporting crossbow

BULLET CROSSBOW *above*
Bullet crossbows were popular from the late 18th century to the early 19th century for both target practice and shooting small game. They had double bowstrings with a pouch in the center for the bullet.

Continued from previous page

A group of 15th-century French crossbowmen shooting from behind pavises

Iron bolt heads

Two 16th-century military bolts

Steel tip

Stirrup (foot strap)

WILLIAM TELL
According to legend, the national hero of Switzerland, William Tell, was forced to shoot an apple from the head of his own son with a crossbow. Tell was being punished for refusing to swear allegiance to the Austrians, who ruled his country in the 1300s.

INCENDIARY (FLAMING) ARROWS
Incendiary arrows and bolts were used in warfare until the 1600s. A wad of hemp or flax was soaked in a flammable substance, fixed beneath the arrowhead, and then lit just before the arrow was shot.

Backsight

BACKSIGHT
Backsights, situated in the middle of bullet and stone crossbows, had a number of apertures (openings) for sighting to different distances. The backsight in this weapon is lying flat and would have been pulled upright for firing.

Double bowstring with leather pouch

Sighting bead

SIGHTING BEAD
A movable sighting bead hung between the foresight pillars of bullet-firing crossbows.

Nock

Axes, daggers, and knives

AXES, DAGGERS, AND KNIVES have been used as weapons since prehistoric times (pp. 6-7). At first, ax heads were made of stone or bronze, but by the Middle Ages they were usually made of steel or iron, and often had additional spikes or projections to make them appear even more formidable. Daggers usually have two sharp edges running into a point and are essentially used for stabbing or cutting. Knives usually have a single-edged blade. By looking at a selection of axes, daggers, and knives from all over the world, it is possible to see how different countries produce blades and shafts to suit their own special requirements and cultures.

19th-century American infantryman carrying a bowie knife

RING KNIFE
Worn as a ring around the user's forefinger, this curved knife can be found amoung the Bantu-speaking peoples of the Lake Turkana region in Tanzania, East Africa.

Ring placed around forefinger

Iron blade

THROWING KNIFE
This African throwing knife (pp. 8-9) comes from Zaire, West Africa. When thrown, the knife turns around its center of gravity so that it will inflict a wound on an opponent whatever its point of impact.

Wooden hilt bound in leather and copper

Worn in palm of hand

STABBING KNIFE *left*
An unusual type of knife, worn in the palm of the hand and then thrust forward by the user. It was made in West Africa by northern Nigerian tribespeople.

STABBING AX *below*
In this unusual-looking ax made by the Matabele people of Zimbabwe, the top of the haft is angled in line with the pointed end of the blade, so the axe can be used with a stabbing as well as a chopping action.

AZTEC DAGGER
The Aztecs, Middle American Indians who once dominated Mexico, made this flint dagger with a mosaic handle.

NAGA WAR AXE *above*
The *dao* is an impressive-looking all-purpose weapon used by the former headhunting peoples from the Naga Hills of Assam, India, in their intertribal warfare.

Long bamboo haft partly bound with rings of plaited cane

FOLDING KNIFE *above*
In this late 19th-century Spanish knife the blade folds back to sit partly within the hilt. The blade was locked into place by a steel spring in the hilt.

Hilt made of horn with brass ferrule

EXECUTIONER'S AX
Executions were usually carried out by single-handed T-shaped axes or, later, by large two-hand axes (left), made only in central and northern Europe.

Plume of dyed animal hair

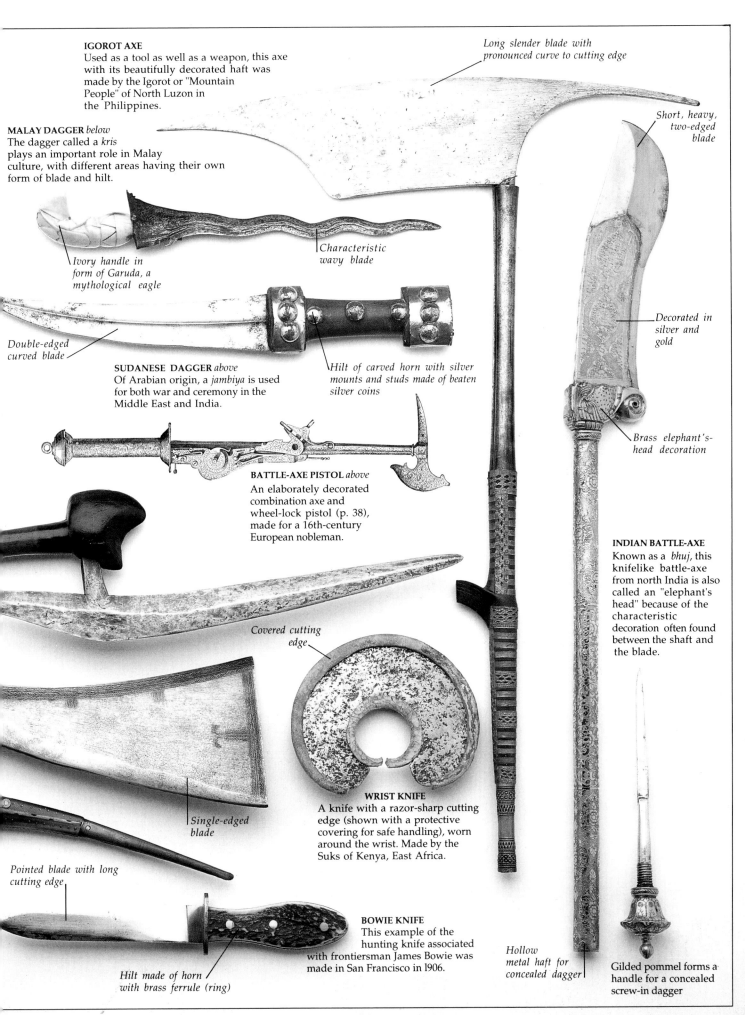

IGOROT AXE
Used as a tool as well as a weapon, this axe with its beautifully decorated haft was made by the Igorot or "Mountain People" of North Luzon in the Philippines.

Long slender blade with pronounced curve to cutting edge

Short, heavy, two-edged blade

MALAY DAGGER *below*
The dagger called a *kris* plays an important role in Malay culture, with different areas having their own form of blade and hilt.

Ivory handle in form of Garuda, a mythological eagle

Characteristic wavy blade

Double-edged curved blade

Decorated in silver and gold

SUDANESE DAGGER *above*
Of Arabian origin, a *jambiya* is used for both war and ceremony in the Middle East and India.

Hilt of carved horn with silver mounts and studs made of beaten silver coins

Brass elephant's-head decoration

BATTLE-AXE PISTOL *above*
An elaborately decorated combination axe and wheel-lock pistol (p. 38), made for a 16th-century European nobleman.

INDIAN BATTLE-AXE
Known as a *bhuj*, this knifelike battle-axe from north India is also called an "elephant's head" because of the characteristic decoration often found between the shaft and the blade.

Covered cutting edge

Single-edged blade

WRIST KNIFE
A knife with a razor-sharp cutting edge (shown with a protective covering for safe handling), worn around the wrist. Made by the Suks of Kenya, East Africa.

Pointed blade with long cutting edge

BOWIE KNIFE
This example of the hunting knife associated with frontiersman James Bowie was made in San Francisco in 1906.

Hilt made of horn with brass ferrule (ring)

Hollow metal haft for concealed dagger

Gilded pommel forms a handle for a concealed screw-in dagger

Mail and plate armour

MAIL - ARMOR MADE from linked iron rings - was probably introduced by the Celts (pp. 10-11) and was common in western Europe until the 14th century. Mail was flexible, so the links did not tear easily. However, a blow could still break bones. Mail also gave poor protection against the increasing use of armor-piercing arrows and sharp weapon points. At first, plate armor (introduced gradually in the 13th century) was simply added to mail armor. But from the 1400s, knights went to war entirely encased in suits of plate armor.

EARLY LEG DEFENSE
An Italian relief, c.1289, showing medieval leather leg protection.

An armored knight in an attitude of devotion, c. 1250

MAIL SHIRT
This Oriental mail shirt is made of solid rings - made without any join. European mail was usually riveted - each ring end flattened and linked by a rivet.

POLEAXE, c. 1580 *right*
This armor-piercing French weapon originally had a longer shaft for use by knights fighting on foot.

MEDIEVAL KNIGHT IN MAIL NECK DEFENSE
Detail from a window in the Palace of Westminster.

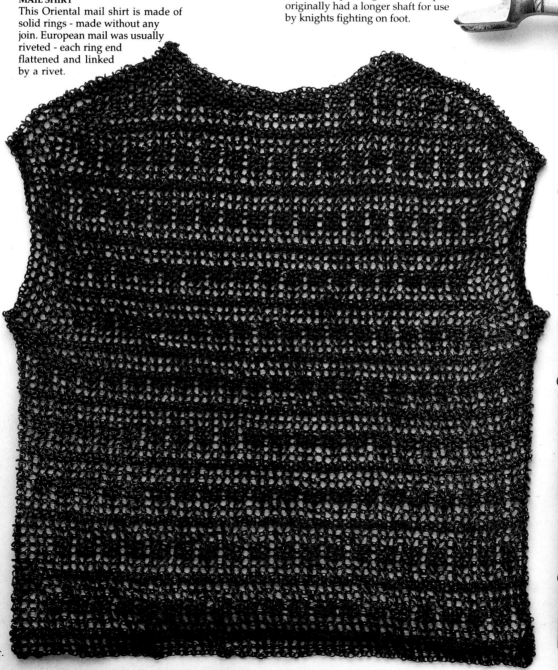

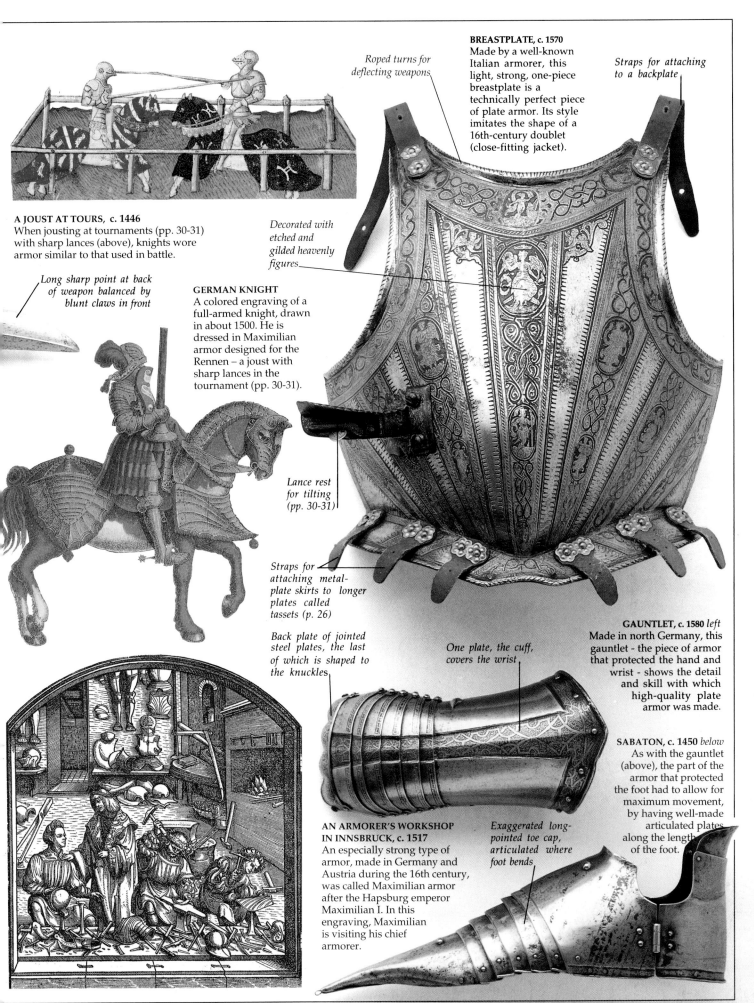

A JOUST AT TOURS, c. 1446
When jousting at tournaments (pp. 30-31) with sharp lances (above), knights wore armor similar to that used in battle.

Roped turns for deflecting weapons

BREASTPLATE, c. 1570
Made by a well-known Italian armorer, this light, strong, one-piece breastplate is a technically perfect piece of plate armor. Its style imitates the shape of a 16th-century doublet (close-fitting jacket).

Straps for attaching to a backplate

Long sharp point at back of weapon balanced by blunt claws in front

GERMAN KNIGHT
A colored engraving of a full-armed knight, drawn in about 1500. He is dressed in Maximilian armor designed for the Rennen – a joust with sharp lances in the tournament (pp. 30-31).

Decorated with etched and gilded heavenly figures

Lance rest for tilting (pp. 30-31)

Straps for attaching metal-plate skirts to longer plates called tassets (p. 26)

Back plate of jointed steel plates, the last of which is shaped to the knuckles

One plate, the cuff, covers the wrist

GAUNTLET, c. 1580 *left*
Made in north Germany, this gauntlet - the piece of armor that protected the hand and wrist - shows the detail and skill with which high-quality plate armor was made.

SABATON, c. 1450 *below*
As with the gauntlet (above), the part of the armor that protected the foot had to allow for maximum movement, by having well-made articulated plates along the length of the foot.

AN ARMORER'S WORKSHOP IN INNSBRUCK, c. 1517
An especially strong type of armor, made in Germany and Austria during the 16th century, was called Maximilian armor after the Hapsburg emperor Maximilian I. In this engraving, Maximilian is visiting his chief armorer.

Exaggerated long-pointed toe cap, articulated where foot bends

25

A suit of armor

By THE MIDDLE OF THE 15TH century, a fully armed knight was virtually encased in plate armor. However, due to the skill of the late medieval armorer, he was not as restricted as he might appear; the armor joints were designed to permit a large amount of movement. The suit of armor on these pages, belonging to a mid-16th-century knight, was made in an Italian workshop - the northern Italians and the southern Germans were the most celebrated armorers in Europe.

13th-century seal of a king of Bohemia, showing the field armor typical of that period

Leather strap and buckle for connecting breastplate to backplate

Vents for breathing

NECK DEFENSE
Gorgets (collar plates) became common in the 15th century.

Upper bevor can be raised with the visor, to get get more air or to eat and drink

Hinge and pivot

PROTECTING THE HEAD *right*
The knight's head was protected by a helmet. This particular type, a close helmet (p. 28), fits to the shape of the face and has connecting neck-guard plates (known as gorget plates).

Lance-rest for stopping the lance from sliding back when striking an opponent

Gorget plates to overlap with gorget

Strap for buckling skirt to tassets

Tassets made of jointed steel plates permitting freedom of movement at the waist

ST. GEORGE KILLING THE DRAGON *left*
Some medieval illustrations of armor were romanticized and inaccurate, as here. However, carefully illustrated manuscripts, brasses, and effigies are very important when looking for depictions of armor, especially for earlier periods from which little survives.

BREASTPLATE SECTION OF CUIRASS
The cuirass, the armor that covered the torso, was made of a breastplate and a backplate connected to each other by straps. Extending from this breastplate are skirts and tassets - armor to protect the abdomen and upper thighs.

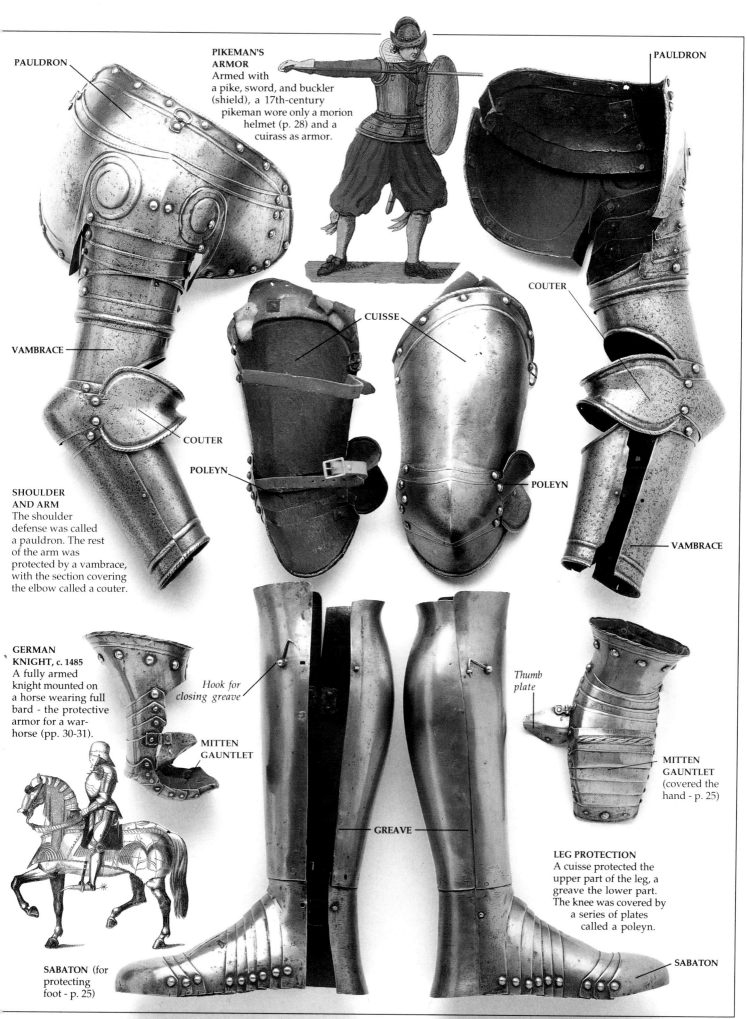

PAULDRON

PAULDRON

PIKEMAN'S ARMOR
Armed with a pike, sword, and buckler (shield), a 17th-century pikeman wore only a morion helmet (p. 28) and a cuirass as armor.

COUTER

CUISSE

VAMBRACE

COUTER

POLEYN

POLEYN

SHOULDER AND ARM
The shoulder defense was called a pauldron. The rest of the arm was protected by a vambrace, with the section covering the elbow called a couter.

VAMBRACE

GERMAN KNIGHT, c. 1485
A fully armed knight mounted on a horse wearing full bard - the protective armor for a war-horse (pp. 30-31).

Hook for closing greave

Thumb plate

MITTEN GAUNTLET

MITTEN GAUNTLET (covered the hand - p. 25)

GREAVE

LEG PROTECTION
A cuisse protected the upper part of the leg, a greave the lower part. The knee was covered by a series of plates called a poleyn.

SABATON (for protecting foot - p. 25)

SABATON

Helmets

WARRIORS HAVE WORN protective helmets since the Bronze Age (pp. 10-11). But in the Middle Ages, helmets became considerably larger so as to give greater protection to the face and neck. The helm was the first all-enclosing helmet, padded inside for comfort, like all helmets, but rather hot to wear. The more open basinet, often with its own visor and mail neckguard, then became popular. From about 1400, a version with plate neck defenses appeared but was rather cumbersome. It was gradually replaced by the side-opening helmet, then the front-opening close helmet. The open, wide-brimmed medieval kettle-hat developed into the morion in the 16th century, and troopers' pots appeared in the 1600s.

FLAT-TOPPED HELM
The German *heaume* or helm was worn by the Crusaders and other European knights from the early 1200s. The one above is a 19th-century reproduction, possibly copied from a manuscript, and has an impractical shape.

13th-century helm with two eye slits and breathing holes

ARCHER, c. 1290 *right*
A mounted archer wearing a conical helm.

Skull

Comb

Lifting peg

Visor with eye slits and breathing vents

High comb

Plume holder

Gorget (neck plate)

Down-turned brim curving up to sharply pointed peak

Originally had leather chin strap tied under chin with lace

CLOSE HELMET, c. 1520-30
The most characteristic helmet of the 16th century was the close helmet (above and left), which unlike earlier helmets was shaped to the chin and had an attached gorget (p. 26).

BURGONE
belo
17th-centur
burgonets had flat brim
and laminated cheekguards

COMB-MORION
A comb-morion was worn by pikemen (as left, but missing the cheekpieces) and musketeers, who found an open style of helmet more convenien when taking aim.

Three pieces of steel welded together

Eye slit

Breathing holes

Stud for attaching visor

CONICAL HELM, c. 1370
After the 1350s, the helm was mainly used for tilting (pp. 30-31). This (19th-century reproduction) late helm would probably have been worn on top of a basinet (right), placing an enormous weight on the knight's shoulders.

Guard-chain or safety chain - when helm not worn, it was often carried by chain

BASINET
Between 1350 and 1450, the most popular type of helmet was the basinet. Visors (hinged plates for protecting the face) were introduced around 1300. In this great basinet of the early 15th century, plates (largely missing except at the neck) replaced the mail curtain.

14th-century knights wearing visored basinets and a common soldier wearing a helmet called a kettle-hat (above)

Neckguard riveted to helmet's skull and partially shaped to neck

Originally covered in cloth, probably velvet

Sliding nasal bar

IRON HAT, c. 1640-50
An unusual helmet is this high-crowned iron hat with a sliding nasal bar, occasionally worn by horsemen during the English Civil War (1642-48). Originally covered in material and with a plume, it looked like a civilian hat of the time.

17th-century musketeer wearing ordinary civilian hat

Face guard formed of three vertical bars

Cheek-pieces

LOBSTER-TAILED POT, c. 1630-50
A type of helmet worn in the mid-17th century originated in Germany, where it was called a *zischagge* (worn by the soldier on the right). It had a laminated neckguard and a sliding noseguard. The English version (shown above and left), was known as the English pot or "lobster-tailed pot." It had a faceguard, neckguard, and hinged cheekpieces.

Tilting armor

THE EARLIEST TOURNAMENTS – mock battles between mounted knights – probably began in the 1100s as a form of rehearsal for war. But by the 1400s, tournaments had evolved into important and colorful social events at which knights displayed their fighting skills and courage before their monarch and their peers. In the 13th century, jousts appeared; two mounted knights charged each other with lances. From about 1430, a barrier (called a tilt) was used, hence the word "tilting." Special armor was made for knights taking part in this and other forms of contest to protect the left (or target) side of the body.

A French knight tilting with a lance

COATS OF ARMS
Tournament contestants were identified by the personal insignia displayed on their shields and tunics. Originally shown on the surcoats worn over mail, the insignia became known as "coats of arms."

PARADE HELMET, c. 1630 *left*
This bronze helmet with its grotesque human face mask was probably used for the parades that took place in 17th-century tournaments, which had become mainly displays of horsemanship.

A JOUSTING CONTEST *above*
By the 16th century, tournaments were accompanied by much formal pageantry. The field, or lists, was enclosed by barriers and overlooked by pavilions where royalty and other notables could watch. This depiction of a tournament shows King Henry VIII tilting with one of his knights, watched by his queen.

TILTING SPUR *below*
Horsemen wear spurs on their heels to urge their horses into action. By the 1500s tilting spurs often had rowels with especially strong and sharp spikes to prod their horses into a charge.

Rowel

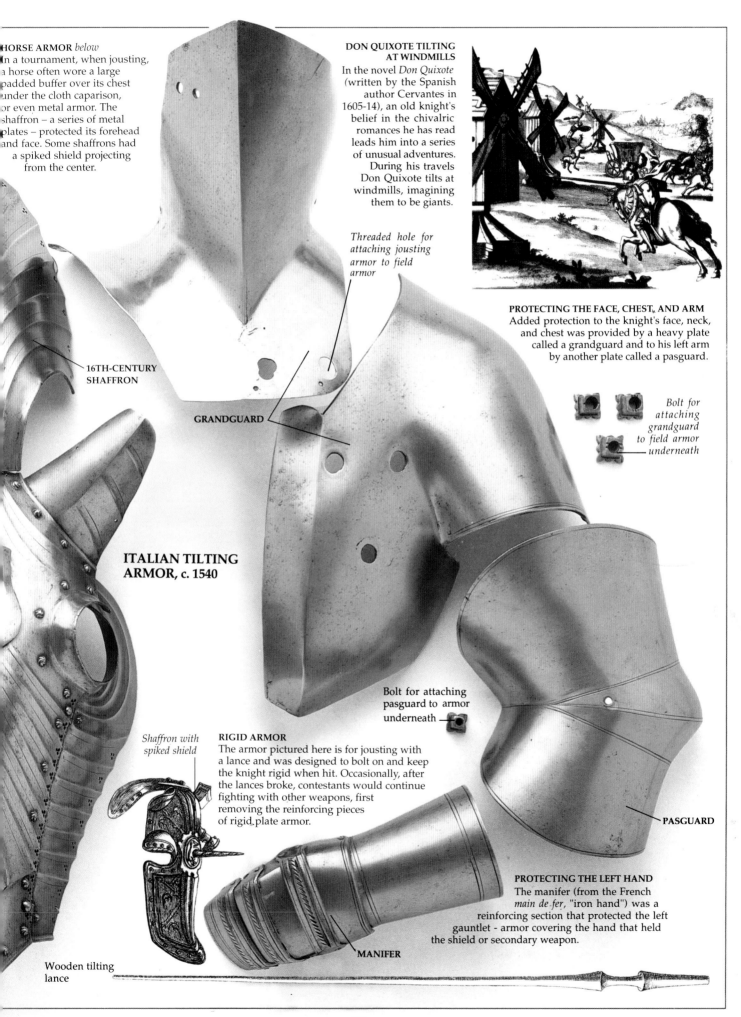

HORSE ARMOR *below*
In a tournament, when jousting, a horse often wore a large padded buffer over its chest under the cloth caparison, or even metal armor. The shaffron – a series of metal plates – protected its forehead and face. Some shaffrons had a spiked shield projecting from the center.

16TH-CENTURY SHAFFRON

DON QUIXOTE TILTING AT WINDMILLS
In the novel *Don Quixote* (written by the Spanish author Cervantes in 1605-14), an old knight's belief in the chivalric romances he has read leads him into a series of unusual adventures. During his travels Don Quixote tilts at windmills, imagining them to be giants.

PROTECTING THE FACE, CHEST, AND ARM
Added protection to the knight's face, neck, and chest was provided by a heavy plate called a grandguard and to his left arm by another plate called a pasguard.

Threaded hole for attaching jousting armor to field armor

Bolt for attaching grandguard to field armor underneath

GRANDGUARD

ITALIAN TILTING ARMOR, c. 1540

Bolt for attaching pasguard to armor underneath

Shaffron with spiked shield

RIGID ARMOR
The armor pictured here is for jousting with a lance and was designed to bolt on and keep the knight rigid when hit. Occasionally, after the lances broke, contestants would continue fighting with other weapons, first removing the reinforcing pieces of rigid plate armor.

PASGUARD

PROTECTING THE LEFT HAND
The manifer (from the French *main de fer*, "iron hand") was a reinforcing section that protected the left gauntlet - armor covering the hand that held the shield or secondary weapon.

MANIFER

Wooden tilting lance

31

An Indian warrior

RECURVED DAGGER
This type of Indian dagger, known as a *khanjar*, has a slightly recurved double-edged blade. The handle is made entirely of steel.

FOR MANY CENTURIES the Persians were the supreme craftsmen of Asia, and oriental arms and armor were dominated by Persian styles and workmanship. In the 16th century, Mogul invaders introduced a Persian style of body armor and weapons to India. Although the Indians had already developed a kind of shield (as seen in early Indian art), and although some Indian weapons, such as the matchlock musket, were derived from European firearms, the arms and armor of the north Indian warrior shown on these pages were remarkably similar to those of a Persian or Turkish warrior.

A 19th-century engraving of a scimitar

Carved ivory grip

Short straight quillons (extended cross guards)

Colored enamel decoration

Double-edged, watered-steel blade

MOGUL BATTLE SCENE *below*
The Moguls were Muslim warriors who founded a great empire in India, which lasted from the 16th to the 19th century. In this 17th-century Mogul miniature, the warriors are wearing characteristic north Indian armor and weapons.

Watered-steel blade

Sling hoops in decorated enamel

Velvet lining

LIGHTWEIGHT SABER *right*
The *shamshir*, a light saber, is a classic Indian sword. Originating in Persia, the weapon spread to India, and eventually to Europe, where it became known as the scimitar.

FIGHTING AXE
A popular weapon among Indian warriors was the *tabar*, an all-steel axe (pp. 34-35). This particular type of *tabar* has a sharp pick opposite a crescent-shaped blade.

CIRCULAR STEEL SHIELD *below*
By the 18th century, Indian and Persian soldiers were using a round shield (*dhal* or *sipar*) made of steel or hide (pp. 34-35). Four bosses (studs) covered the attachment of the handles for carrying the shield on the left arm.

Spike socket (spike missing)

NORTH INDIAN HELMET
Known as a *top,* this Indian helmet had mail curtains called aventails descending to the shoulders. The helmet was secured under the chin with a braid tie.

Socket for feather or tinsel plume (plume missing)

Sliding nasal bar for protecting nose

Aventail to protect the neck, shoulders, and part of the face

INDIAN WARRIORS
Photograph, taken in 1857, of Rajput warriors. They are armed with a *dhal,* *tulwar,* and *bandukh toradar* (matchlock musket).

Made of watered-steel with chiseled and gilded decoration, north Indian, c. 19th century

Mail shoulder straps with metal clasps

ARM GUARD *below*
The tubular vambrace or *dastana* was fastened to the arm with straps. The mail extension is to protect the hand.

RECTANGULAR BREASTPLATE *right*
The Indian cuirass, known as a *char aina* (Persian for "four mirrors"), consisted of a light breastplate, a backplate, and two side plates, all of which were shaped to fit on top of the warrior's mail shirt.

Wooden shamshir scabbard bound in tooled leather

Decorated in gold and silver false damascene

Lined gold damascened trellis pattern

Indian weapons

DESPITE THE FOREIGN INFLUENCE on Indian arms and armor (pp. 32-33), some Indian states and peoples developed specialist weapons of their own which they continued to use up until the beginning of the 20th century, alongside Indo-Persian swords and European-style muskets. These characteristic and often beautifully decorated weapons include the *katar*, the Hindu thrusting dagger, and the *chakram*, the steel war quoit or ring worn by Sikh warriors on their turbans.

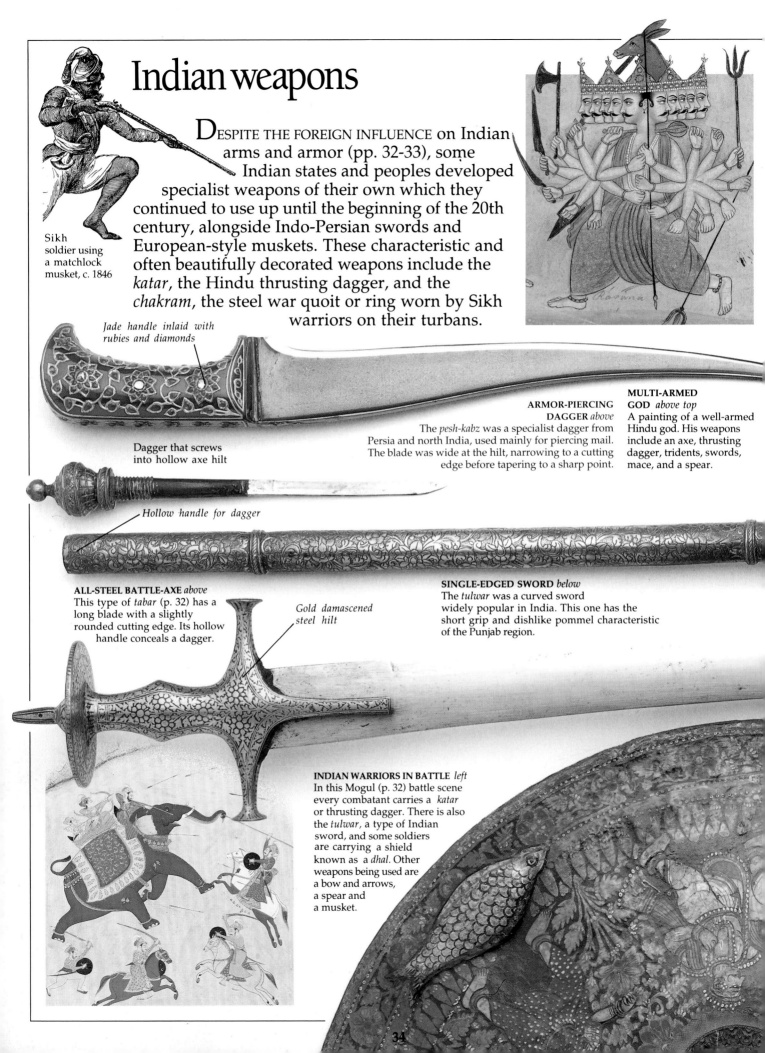

Sikh soldier using a matchlock musket, c. 1846

Jade handle inlaid with rubies and diamonds

Dagger that screws into hollow axe hilt

Hollow handle for dagger

MULTI-ARMED GOD *above top*
A painting of a well-armed Hindu god. His weapons include an axe, thrusting dagger, tridents, swords, mace, and a spear.

ARMOR-PIERCING DAGGER *above*
The *pesh-kabz* was a specialist dagger from Persia and north India, used mainly for piercing mail. The blade was wide at the hilt, narrowing to a cutting edge before tapering to a sharp point.

ALL-STEEL BATTLE-AXE *above*
This type of *tabar* (p. 32) has a long blade with a slightly rounded cutting edge. Its hollow handle conceals a dagger.

Gold damascened steel hilt

SINGLE-EDGED SWORD *below*
The *tulwar* was a curved sword widely popular in India. This one has the short grip and dishlike pommel characteristic of the Punjab region.

INDIAN WARRIORS IN BATTLE *left*
In this Mogul (p. 32) battle scene every combatant carries a *katar* or thrusting dagger. There is also the *tulwar*, a type of Indian sword, and some soldiers are carrying a shield known as a *dhal*. Other weapons being used are a bow and arrows, a spear and a musket.

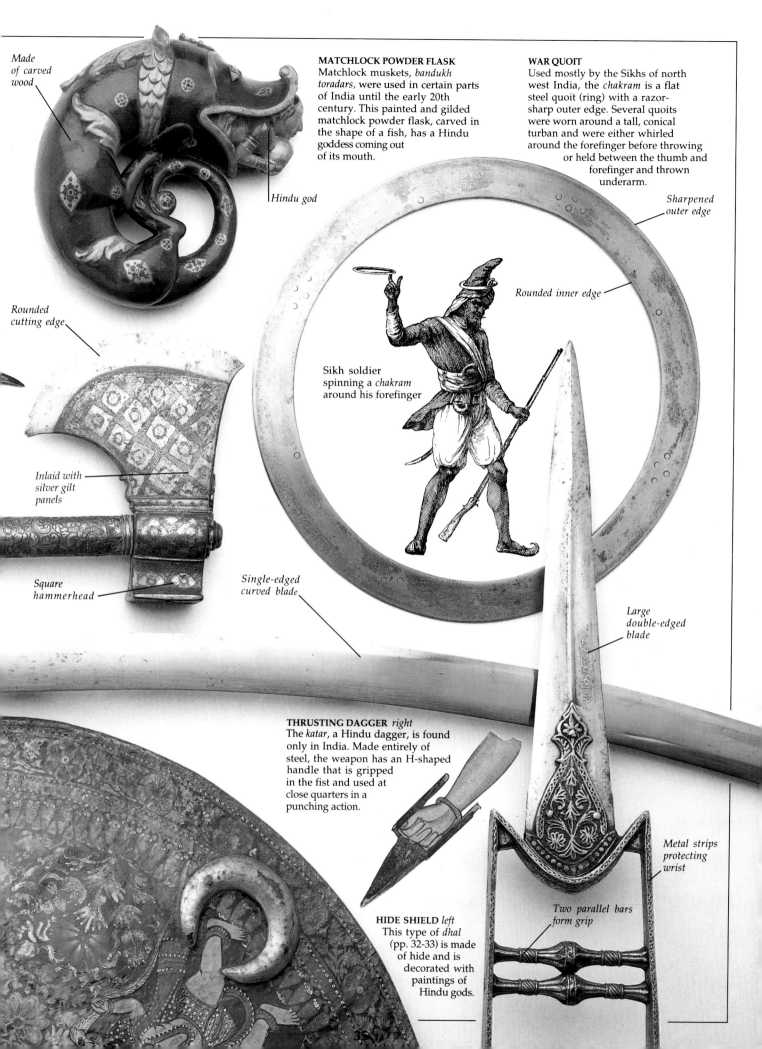

Made
of carved
wood

MATCHLOCK POWDER FLASK
Matchlock muskets, *bandukh toradars*, were used in certain parts of India until the early 20th century. This painted and gilded matchlock powder flask, carved in the shape of a fish, has a Hindu goddess coming out of its mouth.

Hindu god

WAR QUOIT
Used mostly by the Sikhs of north west India, the *chakram* is a flat steel quoit (ring) with a razor-sharp outer edge. Several quoits were worn around a tall, conical turban and were either whirled around the forefinger before throwing or held between the thumb and forefinger and thrown underarm.

Sharpened
outer edge

Rounded inner edge

Rounded
cutting edge

Sikh soldier
spinning a *chakram*
around his forefinger

Inlaid with
silver gilt
panels

Large
double-edged
blade

Square
hammerhead

Single-edged
curved blade

THRUSTING DAGGER *right*
The *katar*, a Hindu dagger, is found only in India. Made entirely of steel, the weapon has an H-shaped handle that is gripped in the fist and used at close quarters in a punching action.

Metal strips
protecting
wrist

Two parallel bars
form grip

HIDE SHIELD *left*
This type of *dhal* (pp. 32-33) is made of hide and is decorated with paintings of Hindu gods.

A Japanese samurai

A *tsuba* (or sword guard)

JAPANESE WEAPONS and armor are unique. Developed over many centuries, the armor is highly decorative, especially the ornamental type worn by the aristocratic warriors known as *samurai* (Japanese for "guard"), whose code of honor dominated Japanese military life from the 12th century until 1868, when the *samurai* class was abolished. Japanese arms are equally well constructed, especially the swords, which are without doubt the finest ever made.

A *wakizashi* scabbard (a *saya*) made of lacquered wood (below)

Wooden sheath for spear head

Metal collar to protect point of junction in a decorative manner

Ornamentation with mosaic design made of mother-of-pearl

Blade made by covering a soft iron core with layers of steel

Flecked lacquer sheath

Lacquered hilt

Known as tsuba, Japanese sword guards are collectors' items (above left)

Hilt made of wood covered with fish skin and bound with flat braid

DAGGER *above*
An example of the typical Japanese dagger (the *tanto*) with its single-edged blade.

SPEAR *left*
Short-bladed spears (*yari*) were carried by horsemen. Foot soldiers carried longer-bladed *yari* (see right).

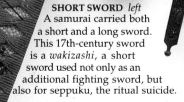

SHORT SWORD *left*
A samurai carried both a short and a long sword. This 17th-century sword is a *wakizashi*, a short sword used not only as an additional fighting sword, but also for seppuku, the ritual suicide.

Large crayfish design in black lacquer

Silken cord for securing sword to girdle

Kabuto *helmet with horn-shaped crest*

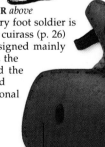

FOOT SOLDIER *above*
This 19th-century foot soldier is wearing a light cuirass (p. 26) or *haramaki*. Designed mainly for foot soldiers, the *haramaki* covered the soldier's chest and sides with additional skirts (*kasazuri*) protecting his lower torso.

SCABBARD FITTINGS
A small knife known as the *kozuka* (left) and a skewer, the *kogai* (far left), were carried on either side of the *tanto* (dagger) and sword scabbards.

Hand guard or half-gauntlet, with leather lining and loops for fingers

36

SAMURAI COMBAT *left*
This early 19th-century print shows a sword fight between two samurai fighting with *katana*, long fighting swords. Their secondary swords, *wakizashi*, are tucked through the girdles around their waists.

Wings or protective flaps known as the *fukigayeshi*

Decorated with brass and lacquer

The maidate - the socket for the helmet crest

Cord for attaching mask to helmet

Hempen mustache

Neckguard (nowdawa) fastened at the back by cords

WAR MASK *above*
Warriors wore different types of war mask or *mempo*, such as this half-mask with a nose-piece. Masks not only secured the helmet firmly to the head, they also gave the wearer a more frightening appearance.

Made of silk overlaid with mail connecting metal plates

Opening (the tehen) for warrior's pigtail to pass through

Helmet bowl (hachi) made of riveted plates

Laminated neck guard (shikoro)

Japanese general wearing a *kabuto* helmet with a helmet crest or *kashira-date*.

SAMURAI HELMET
Known generally as *kabuto*, Japanese helmets developed from prehistoric times until the l9th century, with each period having its own distinct features and design. The *kabuto* was secured to the head with cords attached to the brim.

ARMORED SLEEVE *below*
A type of vambrace (p. 27), the armored sleeve (*kote*) protected the arm from spears and swords. Made of close-fitting material, it was laced over the arm and tied around the chest.

Early firearms

ALTHOUGH GUNPOWDER was used by soldiers in Europe in the 14th century, it was not until the 16th century that small arms began to fulfill their potential. Wooden stocks now helped the firer to aim, absorb the recoil, and hold the hot barrel; an ignition mechanism or lock let him fire at just the right moment. The simple matchlock plunged a smoldering slow-match into the priming pan at the touch of a trigger. A later form of ignition, the wheel-lock, went one stage further, by generating sparks at the moment of firing. As it was too expensive to replace the matchlock entirely for the common soldier, both these systems were used until they were replaced by the more efficient flintlock (pp. 40-41).

HEAVY CAVALRYMAN
Wheel-lock pistols were the first small arms carried by cavalrymen.

Cock or "dog" holding iron pyrites

Brass butt-cap

Stock inlaid with brass and mother-of-pearl

Wheel

Stock shaped to fit wheel

LOADING SEQUENCE
Early muzzleloaders may appear simple, but they had to be loaded in strict sequence to prevent misfiring or personal injury. On the left are a few of the loading and firing actions taught to soldiers using these early firearms.

"March, and with your Musket carry your rest"

"Poise your Musket"

"Shorten your scouring stick"

"Try your Match"

"Give Fire"

The matchlock

This matchlock is a typical infantry musket of the early 17th century. The pan cover was opened just before taking aim. On pulling the trigger, the lock thrust the tip of the match into the pan to ignite the priming, and a flash went through a small touchhole in the barrel wall to set off the main charge.

OBSCURING THE TARGET
One drawback of the original black gunpowder was the dense white smoke it produced, which often obscured the target and made aiming difficult.

Priming pan and cover

Rope slow-match

Wooden stock

Trigger guard

Trigger

GERMAN MATCHLOCK MUSKET,
c. early 17th century

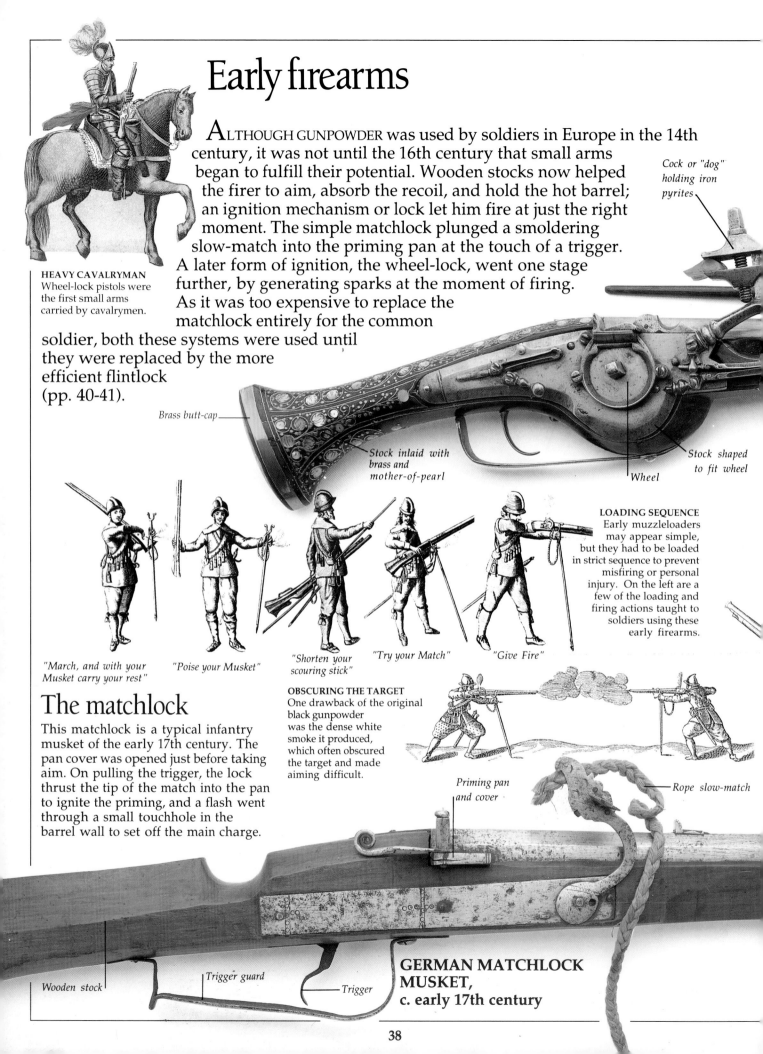

The wheel-lock

This lock produced sparks by holding a bunch of iron pyrites against the notched edge of a spinning wheel, which extended into the bottom of the priming pan. Just below the pan was a square spindle on which a key was fitted. As the key was turned a short chain attached to the mainspring caused it to wind up. After the "dog" or cock was lowered into the pan, the wheel was released. It spun against the pyrites and showered sparks into the pan, setting off the priming and main charge.

RANGE OF FIRE
The advantage of firearms was that they could hit an enemy before he could use a biaded weapon, such as a lance.

Wooden ramrod

Most early small arms were muzzleloaders - loaded from the front or muzzle end

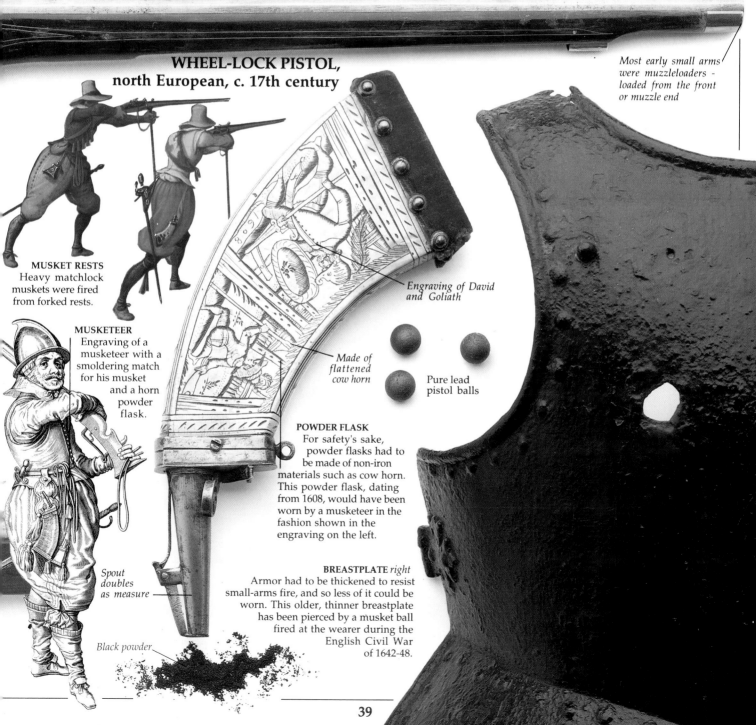

WHEEL-LOCK PISTOL,
north European, c. 17th century

MUSKET RESTS
Heavy matchlock muskets were fired from forked rests.

MUSKETEER
Engraving of a musketeer with a smoldering match for his musket and a horn powder flask.

Spout doubles as measure

Black powder

Engraving of David and Goliath

Made of flattened cow horn

Pure lead pistol balls

POWDER FLASK
For safety's sake, powder flasks had to be made of non-iron materials such as cow horn. This powder flask, dating from 1608, would have been worn by a musketeer in the fashion shown in the engraving on the left.

BREASTPLATE *right*
Armor had to be thickened to resist small-arms fire, and so less of it could be worn. This older, thinner breastplate has been pierced by a musket ball fired at the wearer during the English Civil War of 1642-48.

Flintlock firearms

MORE RELIABLE THAN THE MATCHLOCK and cheaper than the wheel-lock (pp. 38-39), flintlock ignition was used on most European and American firearms from the late 17th century until the l830s. Probably invented in France by Martin Le Bourgeoys in the 1620s, the flintlock mechanism could be set in two positions - one for firing and one for safety. With its basic design improved by only a few details, the flintlock ignition not only dominated the battlefields of all the major wars of that period but was an important civilian weapon as well, used for dueling (pp. 46-47), self-defense (pp. 48-49), and game shooting. Many of these weapons showed the highest standards of craftsmanship.

The pirate Long John Silver in Robert Louis Stevenson's *Treasure Island*

SPORTSMAN SHOOTING GAME
As the hunter fires his flintlock "fowling piece", the flash from the pan can be clearly seen.

Loading and firing a flintlock (also pp. 46-47)

1   Set lock to "half-cock" safety position.
2   Pour correct amount of powder from powder flask (p. 39) or cartridge down barrel.
3   Ram ball, wrapped in its patch (p. 46) or cartridge, down barrel with ramrod.
4   Pour small amount of powder from powder flask into priming pan.
5   Close pan cover.
6   Set lock to "full-cock" position and fire.

Musket ball

MUSKET CARTRIDGE POUCH
Each paper cartridge contains powder and ball for one shot.

Brown walnut stock

Brass butt cap

Lock

Pan cover

Priming pan

Socket

FLINTLOCK MUSKET
This late 18th-century India Pattern musket comes from the family of longarms sometimes known as Brown Bess muskets. These muskets were so strong, simple to use, and relatively reliable, they remained the main British infantry weapon from the 1720s to the 1840s.

SOCKET BAYONET
This bayonet was designed to accompany Brown Bess muskets. Most European and North American armies used triangular-bladed bayonets with a socket to fit over the muzzle.

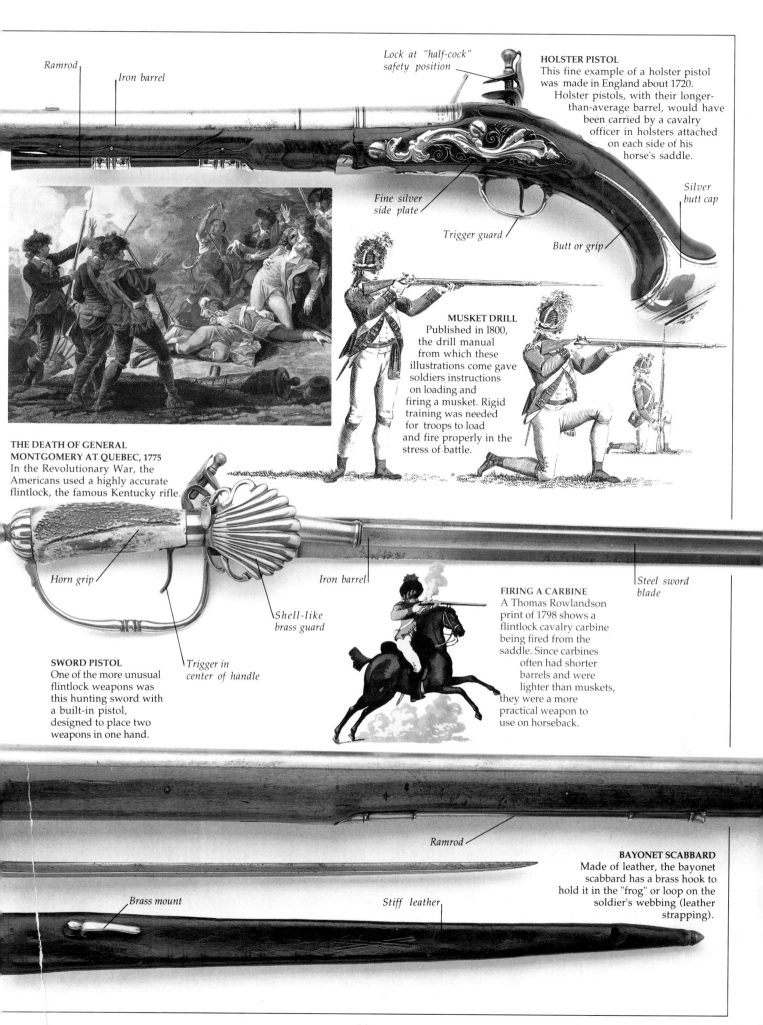

Ramrod

Iron barrel

Lock at "half-cock" safety position

HOLSTER PISTOL
This fine example of a holster pistol was made in England about 1720. Holster pistols, with their longer-than-average barrel, would have been carried by a cavalry officer in holsters attached on each side of his horse's saddle.

Fine silver side plate

Trigger guard

Butt or grip

Silver butt cap

MUSKET DRILL
Published in l800, the drill manual from which these illustrations come gave soldiers instructions on loading and firing a musket. Rigid training was needed for troops to load and fire properly in the stress of battle.

THE DEATH OF GENERAL MONTGOMERY AT QUEBEC, 1775
In the Revolutionary War, the Americans used a highly accurate flintlock, the famous Kentucky rifle.

Horn grip

Iron barrel

Shell-like brass guard

Steel sword blade

SWORD PISTOL
One of the more unusual flintlock weapons was this hunting sword with a built-in pistol, designed to place two weapons in one hand.

Trigger in center of handle

FIRING A CARBINE
A Thomas Rowlandson print of 1798 shows a flintlock cavalry carbine being fired from the saddle. Since carbines often had shorter barrels and were lighter than muskets, they were a more practical weapon to use on horseback.

Ramrod

BAYONET SCABBARD
Made of leather, the bayonet scabbard has a brass hook to hold it in the "frog" or loop on the soldier's webbing (leather strapping).

Brass mount

Stiff leather

Dueling swords

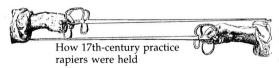

How 17th-century practice rapiers were held

ALTHOUGH THEY WERE FRIGHTENING WEAPONS, the swords taken into battle by medieval knights and foot soldiers were relatively simple (pp. 16-17). However, during the 16th century sword designs changed, and some blades became narrower, longer, and more pointed. These swords, known as rapiers, were designed for well-off gentlemen and aristocrats, not only to defend themselves against casual attacks but also to take part in formal prearranged sword fights known as duels. The art of fighting with a rapier became known as fencing, and as fencing techniques became more sophisticated, sword guards became more complex with the need to protect a civilian's unarmored hand. The greatest swordsmiths of this period came from Toledo in Spain, Milan in Italy, and Solingen in Germany, and many of the weapons they produced are artistically superb examples of the craft of sword making. By the 1650s, rapiers were being replaced as dress swords and dueling swords by a lighter, shorter type of sword with a simpler guard known as a smallsword or court sword. Gentlemen continued to wear smallswords until the end of the 1700s, by which time duels were being fought with pistols (pp. 46-47).

DUELING WITH RAPIERS
An 18th-century drawing by English artist George Cruikshank for a novel called *The Miser's Daughter*. The duel is taking place in Tothill Fields in London, used as dueling grounds for several centuries.

Knuckle guard

RAPIER, c. 1630
In the 1500s, thrusting swords known as rapiers became popular with civilians. Because they had short grips and were impossible to hold with the whole hand, some rapiers had distinctive guards that protected the thumb and forefinger by partly covering the blade.

"THE THREE MUSKETEERS"
The famous historical novel by Alexandre Dumas takes place in France from 1625 to 1665. Wishing to become one of Louis XIII's guardsmen, D'Artagnan involves himself in duels with three famous swordsmen. The joint exploits of D'Artagnan and these three musketeers form the book's narrative.

Guard, known as a pas d'ane, forming two loops that surround the sword's blade

Base of hilt resembling twigs or small branches

Counter-curved quillons (extend cross guards)

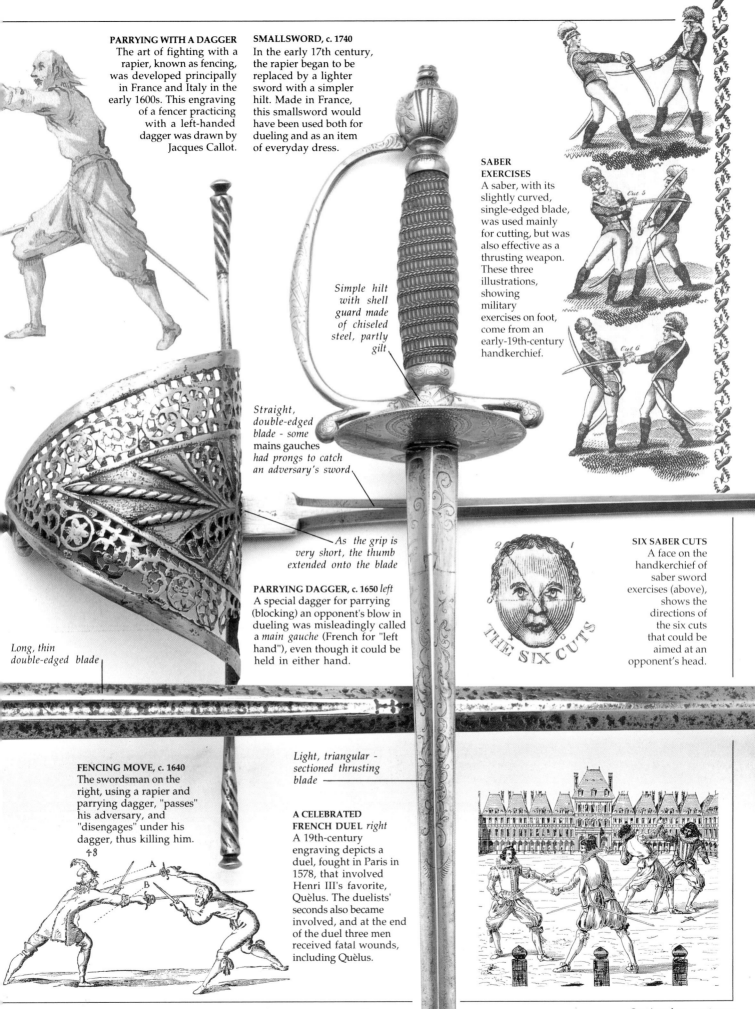

PARRYING WITH A DAGGER
The art of fighting with a rapier, known as fencing, was developed principally in France and Italy in the early 1600s. This engraving of a fencer practicing with a left-handed dagger was drawn by Jacques Callot.

SMALLSWORD, c. 1740
In the early 17th century, the rapier began to be replaced by a lighter sword with a simpler hilt. Made in France, this smallsword would have been used both for dueling and as an item of everyday dress.

SABER EXERCISES
A saber, with its slightly curved, single-edged blade, was used mainly for cutting, but was also effective as a thrusting weapon. These three illustrations, showing military exercises on foot, come from an early-19th-century handkerchief.

Simple hilt with shell guard made of chiseled steel, partly gilt

Straight, double-edged blade - some mains gauches had prongs to catch an adversary's sword

As the grip is very short, the thumb extended onto the blade

PARRYING DAGGER, c. 1650 *left*
A special dagger for parrying (blocking) an opponent's blow in dueling was misleadingly called a *main gauche* (French for "left hand"), even though it could be held in either hand.

Long, thin double-edged blade

SIX SABER CUTS
A face on the handkerchief of saber sword exercises (above), shows the directions of the six cuts that could be aimed at an opponent's head.

THE SIX CUTS

FENCING MOVE, c. 1640
The swordsman on the right, using a rapier and parrying dagger, "passes" his adversary, and "disengages" under his dagger, thus killing him.

Light, triangular-sectioned thrusting blade

A CELEBRATED FRENCH DUEL *right*
A 19th-century engraving depicts a duel, fought in Paris in 1578, that involved Henri III's favorite, Quèlus. The duelists' seconds also became involved, and at the end of the duel three men received fatal wounds, including Quèlus.

43

Continued on next page

PRUSSIAN HUSSARS
The hussar (light cavalryman) on the right is carrying the type of saber that had become the main sword of European light cavalry by the beginning of the 19th century.

SWORD CUTLER'S SHOP, c. 1755
In a Parisian sword cutler's shop, a customer is testing a new blade while workmen near the window are making sword hilts.

BACKSWORD, c.1620
A backsword was a type of military sword used by European cavalry in the 17th century for both cutting and thrusting at an opponent in battle.

Guard for protecting hand, similar to that of rapier

Blade of 17th-century parrying dagger (p. 43)

Blade of 17th-century rapier (pp. 42-43)

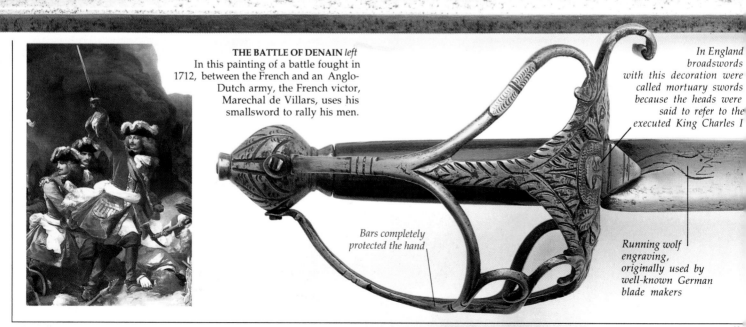

THE BATTLE OF DENAIN *left*
In this painting of a battle fought in 1712, between the French and an Anglo-Dutch army, the French victor, Marechal de Villars, uses his smallsword to rally his men.

In England broadswords with this decoration were called mortuary swords because the heads were said to refer to the executed King Charles I

Bars completely protected the hand

Running wolf engraving, originally used by well-known German blade makers

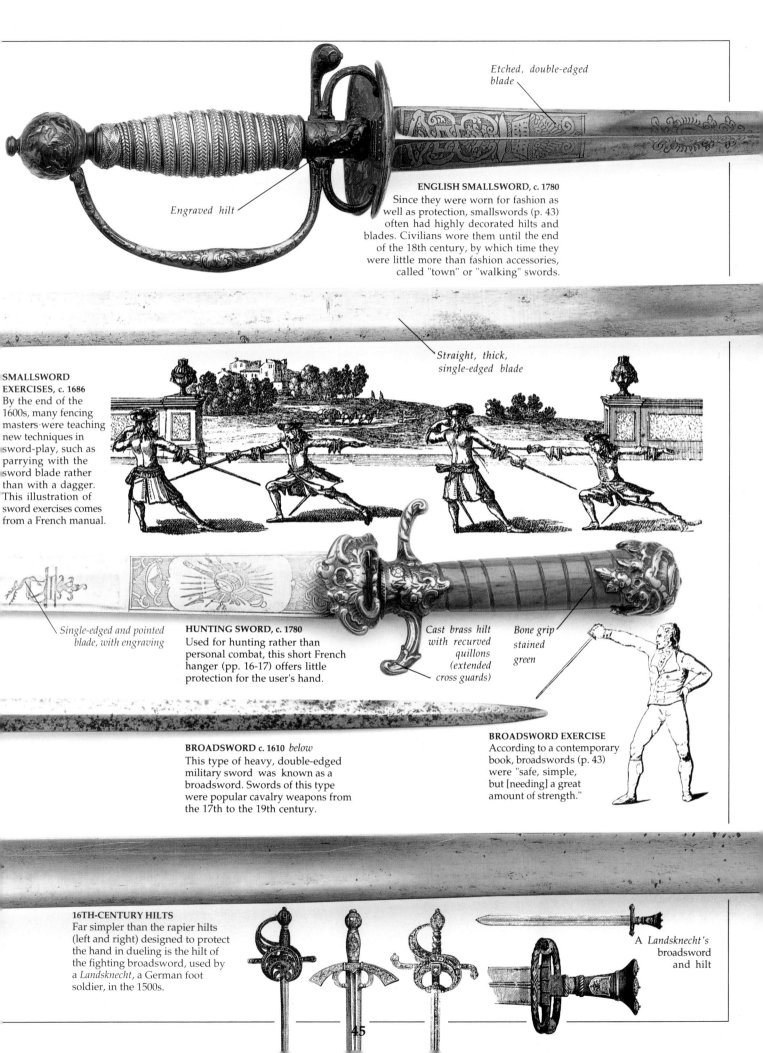

Etched, double-edged blade

ENGLISH SMALLSWORD, c. 1780
Since they were worn for fashion as well as protection, smallswords (p. 43) often had highly decorated hilts and blades. Civilians wore them until the end of the 18th century, by which time they were little more than fashion accessories, called "town" or "walking" swords.

Engraved hilt

SMALLSWORD EXERCISES, c. 1686
By the end of the 1600s, many fencing masters were teaching new techniques in sword-play, such as parrying with the sword blade rather than with a dagger. This illustration of sword exercises comes from a French manual.

Straight, thick, single-edged blade

HUNTING SWORD, c. 1780
Used for hunting rather than personal combat, this short French hanger (pp. 16-17) offers little protection for the user's hand.

Single-edged and pointed blade, with engraving

Cast brass hilt with recurved quillons (extended cross guards)

Bone grip stained green

BROADSWORD EXERCISE
According to a contemporary book, broadswords (p. 43) were "safe, simple, but [needing] a great amount of strength."

BROADSWORD c. 1610 *below*
This type of heavy, double-edged military sword was known as a broadsword. Swords of this type were popular cavalry weapons from the 17th to the 19th century.

16TH-CENTURY HILTS
Far simpler than the rapier hilts (left and right) designed to protect the hand in dueling is the hilt of the fighting broadsword, used by a *Landsknecht*, a German foot soldier, in the 1500s.

A Landsknecht's broadsword and hilt

Dueling pistols

Aᴌᴛʜᴏᴜɢʜ ɪʟʟᴇɢᴀʟ, for centuries dueling was a popular way for "gentlemen" and army officers to settle their quarrels. By the late 18th century, when flintlock pistols were perfected, they had replaced swords (pp. 42-43) as the preferred method of fighting a duel. Gunsmiths began to make special dueling pistols in matched pairs, which they supplied fitted into a case with all the necessary accessories for both making the bullets and cleaning and loading the pistols. In order for dueling pistols to be as accurate as possible, the pistols were of the highest quality, with added refinements such as sights and special triggers. All dueling pistols were muzzle-loaders (pp. 38-39), and until about 1820-30 all used flintlock ignition.

THE END OF THE DUELING ERA
A French duelist, c. 1887. His opponent is shown far left. Standing side-on presented a smaller target.

Spring-loaded trigger

SENSITIVE TRIGGER *above*
Many dueling pistols had a special "hair" or "set" trigger, worked by an extra spring in the lock. These light triggers allowed the user to fire the pistol without disturbing his aim.

The grip - part of stock where pistol is held

The butt - rear part of stock

Wooden end for holding ramrod

WOODEN STOCK *right*
In all dueling pistols the wooden stock was carefully made so that the butt would fit comfortably in the duelist's hand. Some pistols had a squarer saw-handled butt to assist the grip.

Making a bullet

The lead ball or bullet was made at home by the firer, using a bullet mold provided with the pistol. Lead was melted over a fire and poured into the mold. After a few seconds the scissor-like mold was opened and the ball shaken out. Excess lead or "sprue" was cut off with the shears, which were part of the mold handles.

Black gunpowder

Lead bullets

LINEN PATCH
To fit tightly in the barrel, the bullet was wrapped in a cloth or leather patch.

ALEKSANDR PUSHKIN
Eminent men who took part in duels included the Duke of Wellington, a British general and statesman, and the French politician Georges Clemenceau. A famous victim was the great Russian writer Pushkin, killed in a duel with his wife's lover in 1837.

Nozzle forms a measure

RAMROD
A wood or metal ramrod (kept in a recess below the barrel) was used to push the ball and patch down the bore. Many ramrods had special attachments for cleaning out the bore.

BULLET MOLD
Bullets were made by pouring melted lead into the hollow chamber of the bullet mold (p. 57).

POWDER FLASK
Gunpowder was kept in a powder flask. Originally made of wood or horn (p. 39), by the 19th century most powder flasks were made of metal. When self-contained cartridges were introduced, powder flasks became obsolete.

Metal end for ramming bullet down bore

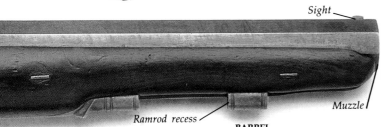

AMERICAN ANTI-DUELING CARTOON, c. 1821 *left*
When this anti-dueling cartoon was published in Philadelphia, dueling was as popular in America as it was in France and England.

AN AFFAIR OF HONOR, c. 1820
Duels were called "affairs of honor." A gentleman who considered himself insulted by the behavior of another would challenge him to a duel. To refuse to be "called out" cast a bad slur on a gentleman's honor. The English artist Robert Cruikshank painted this duel at the height of the dueling era.

Sight

Muzzle

Ramrod recess

BARREL
Dueling pistols were muzzle-loaders (pp. 38-39). The outside of the barrel was usually octagonal in shape and fitted with sights.

A PAIR OF ENGLISH DUELING PISTOLS, c. 1800 (lock of lower pistol shown separately)

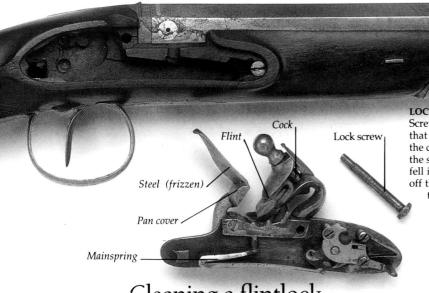

Cock

Flint

Lock screw

Steel (frizzen)

Pan cover

Mainspring

LOCK *left*
Screwed to the side of the stock, the lock was the mechanism that fired the pistol. When the trigger of a flintlock was pulled, the cock swung forward, making sparks by scraping the flint down the steel (or frizzen) and pushing open the pan cover. The sparks fell into the priming powder, which burned with a flash and set off the main powder charge in the barrel through the small touchhole.

THE RULES OF DUELING
In pistol duels combatants had to follow a strict set of rules. The exact rules of the fight were agreed between the two men and their "seconds" - friends who loaded the pistols and witnessed the duel. Usually, the two duelists stood an agreed number of paces apart, with their pistols pointing at the ground. At a given signal, such as the dropping of a hand-kerchief by one of the seconds, the duelists raised their pistols and fired.

Cleaning a flintlock

1 Extract any unfired ball and powder from barrel using a special cleaning rod or tool attached to the ramrod.
2 Clean and oil empty barrel with cloth attached to ramrod or cleaning rod.
3 Brush away burned gunpowder in and around priming pan.
4 Oil lock.   5 Replace flint if worn out.

Oil can for oiling lock and barrel

A nonfatal duel, fought in France in 1893

Spare flints

PAN BRUSH
The priming pan needed frequent cleaning.

FLINTS AND LEATHERS
Leather was used to grip the flint in the jaws of the lock.

TURNSCREW
A turnscrew was used for removing the lock.

Attack by highwaymen

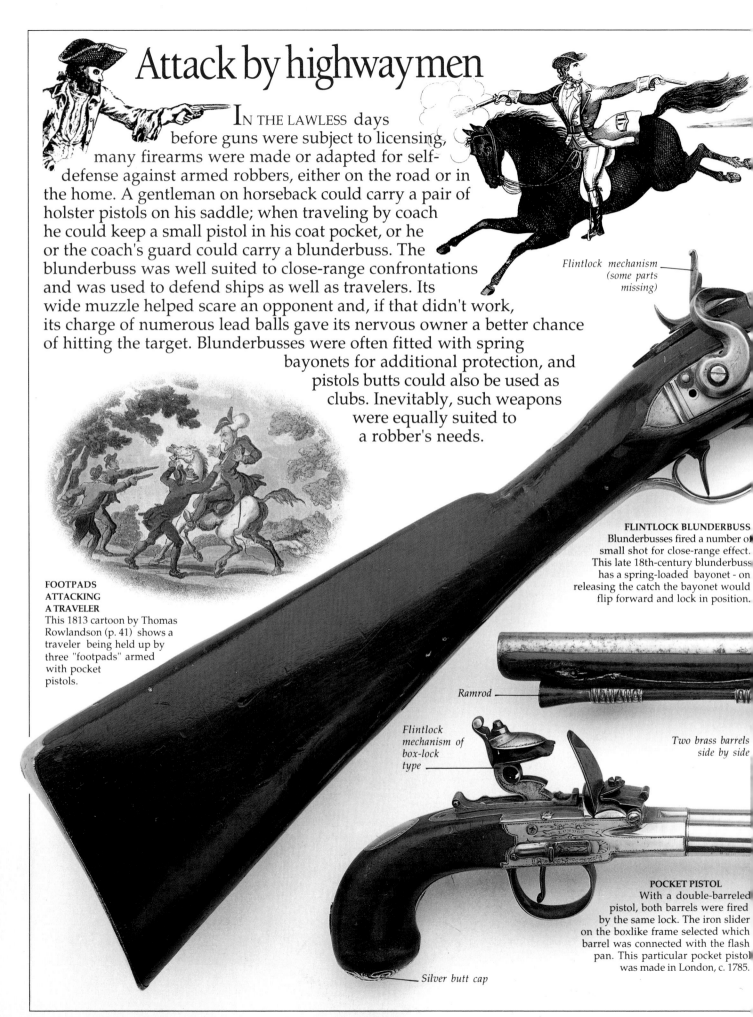

IN THE LAWLESS days before guns were subject to licensing, many firearms were made or adapted for self-defense against armed robbers, either on the road or in the home. A gentleman on horseback could carry a pair of holster pistols on his saddle; when traveling by coach he could keep a small pistol in his coat pocket, or he or the coach's guard could carry a blunderbuss. The blunderbuss was well suited to close-range confrontations and was used to defend ships as well as travelers. Its wide muzzle helped scare an opponent and, if that didn't work, its charge of numerous lead balls gave its nervous owner a better chance of hitting the target. Blunderbusses were often fitted with spring bayonets for additional protection, and pistols butts could also be used as clubs. Inevitably, such weapons were equally suited to a robber's needs.

Flintlock mechanism (some parts missing)

FOOTPADS ATTACKING A TRAVELER
This 1813 cartoon by Thomas Rowlandson (p. 41) shows a traveler being held up by three "footpads" armed with pocket pistols.

FLINTLOCK BLUNDERBUSS
Blunderbusses fired a number of small shot for close-range effect. This late 18th-century blunderbuss has a spring-loaded bayonet - on releasing the catch the bayonet would flip forward and lock in position.

Ramrod

Flintlock mechanism of box-lock type

Two brass barrels side by side

POCKET PISTOL
With a double-barreled pistol, both barrels were fired by the same lock. The iron slider on the boxlike frame selected which barrel was connected with the flash pan. This particular pocket pistol was made in London, c. 1785.

Silver butt cap

Partially opened
spring bayonet

Bayonet
catch

Bayonet spring
and lock

DICK TURPIN *left*
During the l730s Dick Turpin, the legendary highwayman, was the most wanted man in England. Here Turpin is shown improbably firing two pistols in opposite directions, while jumping a tollgate on his famous horse, Black Bess.

Brass barrel

Ramrod

TRICORN HAT
A three-cornered or tricorn hat would have been worn by the more respectable 18th-century highwayman.

ROBERT MACAIRE
During the 18th century celebrated highwaymen soon became folk heroes. Here, a notorious robber called Robert Macaire is being portrayed by an actor named Mr. Hicks.

HOLSTER PISTOL
The butt cap of this early 18th-century holster pistol allowed the pistol to be reversed and used as a club once the single shot had been fired.

Brass mounted

Butt cap

AN ATTACK BY HIGHWAYMEN
In 1750 two highwaymen robbed Lord Eglinton, who was riding in his carriage near London. On this occasion the blunderbuss his lordship is holding proved useless.

Bizarre hand weapons

THROUGHOUT recorded history extraordinary and seemingly impractical weapons have been made alongside conventional swords, guns, and bows and arrows. The unusual weapons shown on these pages prove that many local and tribal weapons were just as ingenious and deadly as the specialist weapons devised for close-range attack and defense, or the strange-looking combination pistols made by gunsmiths for their rich customers.

ITALIAN GUNNER'S STILETTO *below*
The engraving on the blade of this 18th-century dagger is a numbered scale for artillery commanders to calculate the bore size of cannons.

Engraved blade

"CROW'S FEET" c. 19th century *left*
First used in the 4th century B.C., caltrops or "crow's feet" are made of four or more sharp iron spikes. They were thrown in front of horse's hooves or infantrymen's feet.

Single-edged curved blade

THE LAST ARMOR *below*
In the 1700s and 1800s, the only piece of armor regularly worn by European or American infantry was the gorget (p. 26), worn as a mark of rank for officers rather than for defense. Today, gorgets are still used with full dress in some countries. This particular gorget (below) belonged to an officer of the marines in the British navy, c. 1800.

Dagger blade

Gorget

Trigger

Barrel concealed in brass handle

Weapon fired when turned muzzle plugs were removed

CUTLERY PISTOLS *right*
Among the most impractical flintlock firearms ever devised must be this companion knife and fork, made in Germany about 1740.

GURKHA KNIFE *right*
The *kukri* is the national knife and principal weapon of the Gurkhas of Nepal. Although the *kukri* is useful for cutting through jungle, its heavy, curved blade also makes it a deadly fighting weapon.

INDIAN MACE *right*
This all-steel mace was made in India in the 19th century. The owner would have used the mace to lean on while he was sitting down but could have quickly clubbed any possible enemy with the metal "hand."

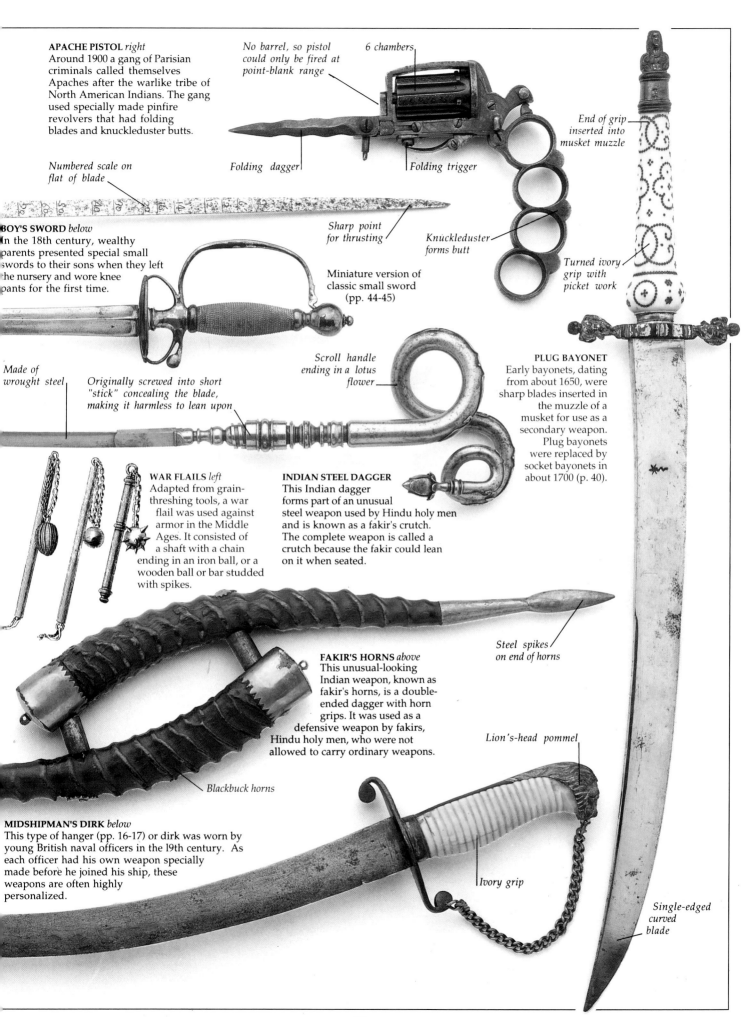

APACHE PISTOL *right*
Around 1900 a gang of Parisian criminals called themselves Apaches after the warlike tribe of North American Indians. The gang used specially made pinfire revolvers that had folding blades and knuckleduster butts.

No barrel, so pistol could only be fired at point-blank range

6 chambers

End of grip inserted into musket muzzle

Folding dagger

Folding trigger

Numbered scale on flat of blade

Sharp point for thrusting

Knuckleduster forms butt

Turned ivory grip with picket work

BOY'S SWORD *below*
In the 18th century, wealthy parents presented special small swords to their sons when they left the nursery and wore knee pants for the first time.

Miniature version of classic small sword (pp. 44-45)

Made of wrought steel

Originally screwed into short "stick" concealing the blade, making it harmless to lean upon

Scroll handle ending in a lotus flower

PLUG BAYONET
Early bayonets, dating from about 1650, were sharp blades inserted in the muzzle of a musket for use as a secondary weapon. Plug bayonets were replaced by socket bayonets in about 1700 (p. 40).

WAR FLAILS *left*
Adapted from grain-threshing tools, a war flail was used against armor in the Middle Ages. It consisted of a shaft with a chain ending in an iron ball, or a wooden ball or bar studded with spikes.

INDIAN STEEL DAGGER
This Indian dagger forms part of an unusual steel weapon used by Hindu holy men and is known as a fakir's crutch. The complete weapon is called a crutch because the fakir could lean on it when seated.

Steel spikes on end of horns

FAKIR'S HORNS *above*
This unusual-looking Indian weapon, known as fakir's horns, is a double-ended dagger with horn grips. It was used as a defensive weapon by fakirs, Hindu holy men, who were not allowed to carry ordinary weapons.

Lion's-head pommel

Blackbuck horns

MIDSHIPMAN'S DIRK *below*
This type of hanger (pp. 16-17) or dirk was worn by young British naval officers in the l9th century. As each officer had his own weapon specially made before he joined his ship, these weapons are often highly personalized.

Ivory grip

Single-edged curved blade

Grenadiers and cavalry

By THE TIME Napoleon Bonaparte was conquering most of Europe at the beginning of the 1800s, flintlock firearms - muskets, carbines, and pistols - had become the chief weapons of armies in both Europe and North America (pp. 40-41). Among the specialist flintlocks were grenade launchers - weapons for destroying defensive works such as doorways and barricades. Originally grenades were used by specially trained troops called grenadiers. But by the 19th century most so-called grenadiers were ordinary infantry corps who used flintlock muskets rather than grenades. In the Napoleonic Wars (1796-1815) muskets proved such unbeatable weapons that they often destroyed the effectiveness of mounted troops, who relied more on swords and lances than firearms.

FRENCH GRENADIER
Despite his title, the main weapon of this soldier in the French Light Infantry was his flintlock musket.

GRENADIER'S POUCH AND BELT
An 18th-century English grenadier's pouch decorated with a one-legged grenadier. Grenadiers of this period wore special pointed caps to enable them to throw grenades overarm.

Brass match case

Brush for removing excess gunpowder

Velvet pouch

Grenade

Grenade pouch

Live grenade

Buff leather belt

Iron case

Charge hole

Fuse

Early hand grenade

Lighted match

Gunstock

LATE 18TH-CENTURY BRITISH ARMY PATTERN GRENADE THROWER. WEIGHT 11 LBS (5 KILOS)

LOVE AND HONOUR

Single-edged blade

SOLDIER LIGHTING GRENADE *left*
By the late 1600s small bombs known as hand grenades were commonly used in European battles. Early grenades were hollow iron balls filled with black gunpowder. Holes were bored through the wall of the grenade (below left) and threaded with a short fuse.

GRENADE LAUNCHER
This fearsome weapon, designed to increase the range of grenades, first appeared in the 16th century. Any mistake in lighting the grenade fuse was liable to cause fatal injuries to the grenadier and anybody nearby.

16 ins (40 cm) long barrel

CAVALRY CHARGE
At the Battle of Waterloo in 1815, a series of classic encounters took place as the French cavalry charged the British infantry squares. While one line of the British square fired a volley, another line reloaded. In this battle, the inability of the French cavalry to break through these squares proved decisive.

Fleur-de-lis

CAVALRY SWORD
Late 18th-century French saber with a brass hilt decorated with a fleur-de-lis, the royal emblem of France. The sword has a single-edged, straight blade.

BRITISH OFFICER'S SHAKO, EARLY 19TH CENTURY

Basket hilt protects the entire hand

Engraving reads Pro Deo fide et Patria - "For God, Faith and Country"

Napoleon Bonaparte in 1812

CUIRASSIER'S SWORD
French saber with the gilded brass hilt and slightly curved blade of the type used by cuirassier or heavy cavalry regiments in Napoleon's army.

OFFICER'S SHAKO
In the 1800s shakos, stiff peaked caps, were worn in many armies (also top of opposite page).

Keeping law and order

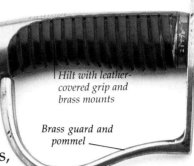

Sɪɴᴄᴇ ᴛʜᴇ ᴡᴏʀᴅ "ᴘᴏʟɪᴄᴇ" ᴍᴇᴀɴꜱ different types of forces in different countries - civilian and military, uniformed and plain-clothed - the batons, rattles, and other law-enforcement equipment shown on these pages are best described as weapons for combating crime and keeping public order. All of them were in use during the 19th century, and when it is considered how much violent crime and civilian unrest took place during the 1800s, these weapons seem hardly sufficent.

Of course, more powerful weapons were issued to some police forces of necessity - by the late 19th century the Berlin police were armed with swords, pistols, and brass knuckles, and the police in New York and Boston first used firearms during the 1850s. But in most European and American towns the increasing respect felt for the ordinary civilian law-enforcement officer was due in part to his being so lightly armed.

LONDON POLICEMAN
A late 19th-century policeman goes on night patrol with just a truncheon and a lamp.

Hilt with leather-covered grip and brass mounts

Brass guard and pommel

Brass mount

Originally had a wooden clapper that made a penetrating sound

Lead weights gave extra weight when swung

POLICE RATTLES
Lead weights in a rattle (above) made it a useful weapon as well as giving it extra weight when it was swung. Rattles with clappers (right) made an especially loud noise.

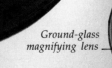

PICTUREBOOK POLICEMAN
The fact that images of 19th-century policemen were often used to frighten children into behaving properly is well illustrated by this picture of a policeman in a child's gift book dating from 1867.

POLICE WHISTLE *right*
Whistles were adopted in many police forces during the 19th century when it was found that they could be heard over far greater distances than the sound from a rattle.

Buckle for securing at the back of neck

LEATHER COLLAR
In some early police forces officers wore leather collars called stocks to protect them from being garroted - strangled with a cord. Stocks were both hot and restrictive to wear.

Stock is 4 ins (10 cms) wide

Twin handles

Outer tin shell

Ground-glass magnifying lens

BULLSEYE LANTERN
The standard British police lamp in the 19th century, the bullseye lantern hooked onto the belt the policeman wore over his greatcoat.

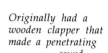

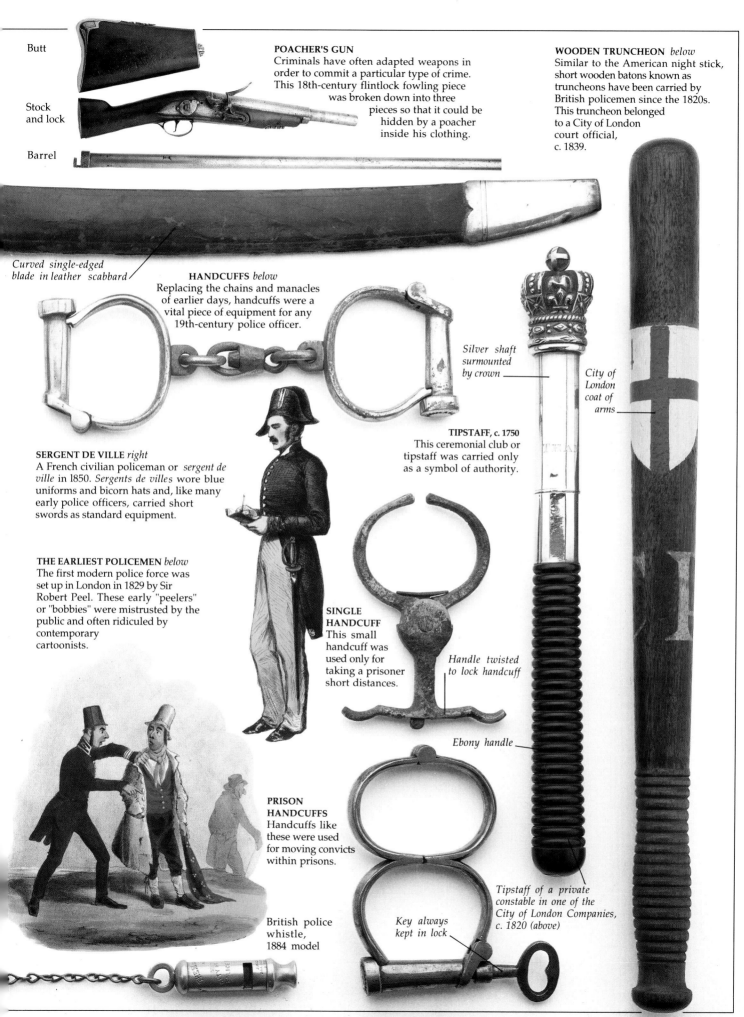

Butt

Stock
and lock

Barrel

POACHER'S GUN
Criminals have often adapted weapons in
order to commit a particular type of crime.
This 18th-century flintlock fowling piece
was broken down into three
pieces so that it could be
hidden by a poacher
inside his clothing.

WOODEN TRUNCHEON *below*
Similar to the American night stick,
short wooden batons known as
truncheons have been carried by
British policemen since the 1820s.
This truncheon belonged
to a City of London
court official,
c. 1839.

*Curved single-edged
blade in leather scabbard*

HANDCUFFS *below*
Replacing the chains and manacles
of earlier days, handcuffs were a
vital piece of equipment for any
19th-century police officer.

*Silver shaft
surmounted
by crown*

*City of
London
coat of
arms*

SERGENT DE VILLE *right*
A French civilian policeman or *sergent de
ville* in l850. *Sergents de villes* wore blue
uniforms and bicorn hats and, like many
early police officers, carried short
swords as standard equipment.

TIPSTAFF, c. 1750
This ceremonial club or
tipstaff was carried only
as a symbol of authority.

THE EARLIEST POLICEMEN *below*
The first modern police force was
set up in London in 1829 by Sir
Robert Peel. These early "peelers"
or "bobbies" were mistrusted by the
public and often ridiculed by
contemporary
cartoonists.

**SINGLE
HANDCUFF**
This small
handcuff was
used only for
taking a prisoner
short distances.

*Handle twisted
to lock handcuff*

Ebony handle

**PRISON
HANDCUFFS**
Handcuffs like
these were used
for moving convicts
within prisons.

*Tipstaff of a private
constable in one of the
City of London Companies,
c. 1820 (above)*

British police
whistle,
1884 model

*Key always
kept in lock*

The percussion revolver

PERCUSSION IGNITION was an important development in the history of firearms. In the early 19th century it offered instant ignition and greatly improved resistance to wet weather. In its most common form a thimble-cap containing an explosive compound was placed on a steel nipple. When struck by the weapon's hammer the cap exploded, sending a jet of flame through the nipple into the powder charge. Early percussion guns were still muzzleloaders (pp. 38-39), with the cap separate from the powder and ball. Later, the cap was incorporated in the base of a self-contained metallic cartridge, with the powder and ball. The metal case sealed in the explosive gases, allowing efficient breech-loading designs that are still in world-wide use today.

SHERLOCK HOLMES
An actor portraying the most famous detective in literature, Sherlock Holmes, is shown holding a smoking percussion pistol.

PERCUSSION REVOLVER
A percussion revolver, c.1855, made by the English gunmaker William Tranter. This self-cocking double-action design could be used with one hand. Pulling the lower trigger turned the cylinder and cocked the hammer; pulling the upper trigger fired the shot.

Back sight

Five-shot revolving cylinder

Hammer or cock

Nipple

Button for opening gun at axis

Linen tape to close bag

Linen bag

Upper trigger

Lower trigger

INDIAN MUTINY, 1857 *below*
In the kind of hand-to-hand fighting that took place in the Indian Mutiny, British officers preferred self-cocking revolvers (like the Tranter), for rapid firing.

BAG OF CARTRIDGES
To load the revolver, the copper cover was removed from the paper sachet of powder attached to the bullet, and the cartridge was loaded into the front of the revolver cylinder. The revolver would have been equipped with a detachable rammer.

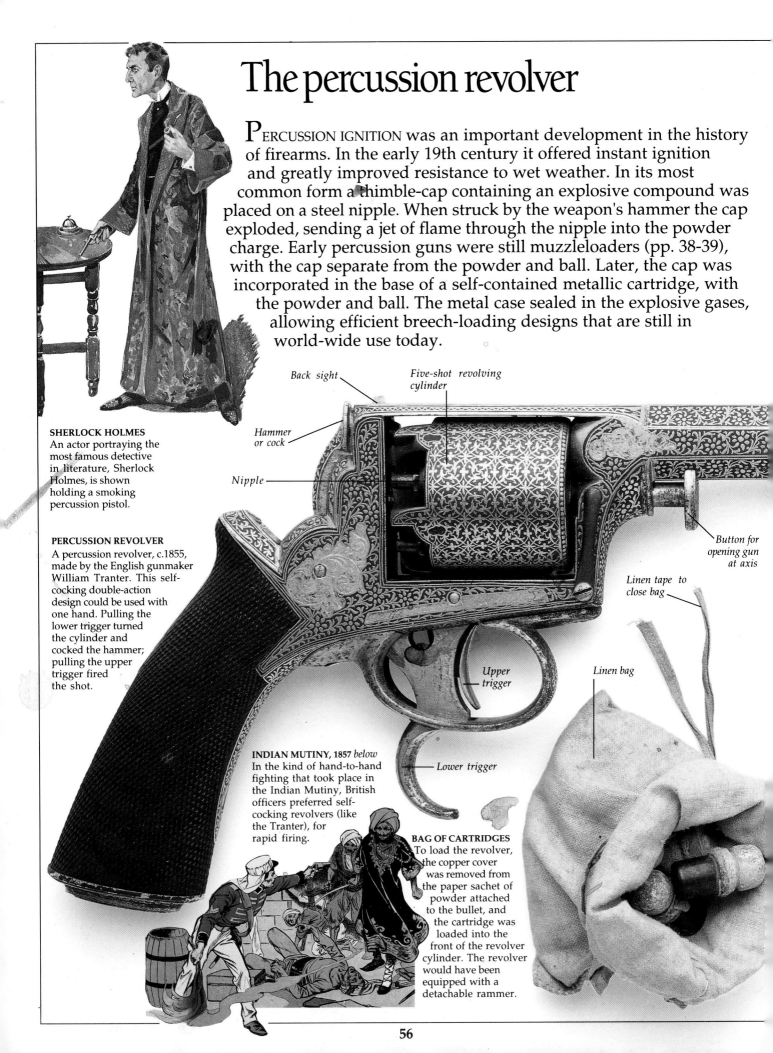

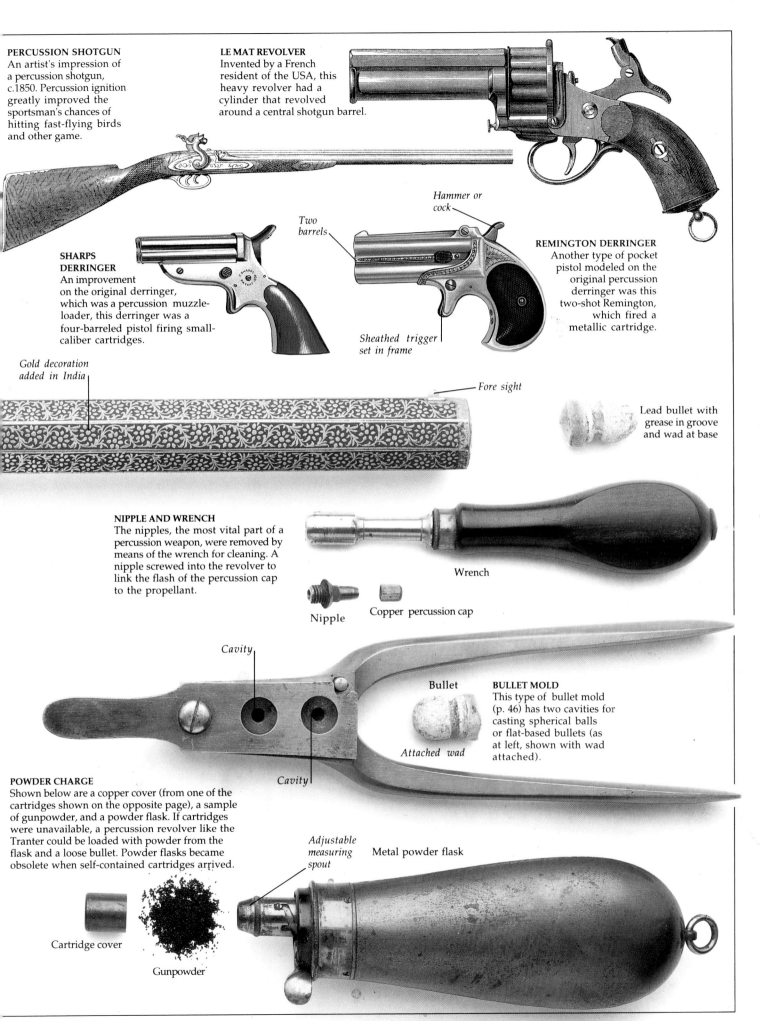

PERCUSSION SHOTGUN
An artist's impression of a percussion shotgun, c.1850. Percussion ignition greatly improved the sportsman's chances of hitting fast-flying birds and other game.

LE MAT REVOLVER
Invented by a French resident of the USA, this heavy revolver had a cylinder that revolved around a central shotgun barrel.

Hammer or cock

Two barrels

SHARPS DERRINGER
An improvement on the original derringer, which was a percussion muzzle-loader, this derringer was a four-barreled pistol firing small-caliber cartridges.

REMINGTON DERRINGER
Another type of pocket pistol modeled on the original percussion derringer was this two-shot Remington, which fired a metallic cartridge.

Sheathed trigger set in frame

Gold decoration added in India

Fore sight

Lead bullet with grease in groove and wad at base

NIPPLE AND WRENCH
The nipples, the most vital part of a percussion weapon, were removed by means of the wrench for cleaning. A nipple screwed into the revolver to link the flash of the percussion cap to the propellant.

Wrench

Nipple

Copper percussion cap

Cavity

Bullet

BULLET MOLD
This type of bullet mold (p. 46) has two cavities for casting spherical balls or flat-based bullets (as at left, shown with wad attached).

Attached wad

Cavity

POWDER CHARGE
Shown below are a copper cover (from one of the cartridges shown on the opposite page), a sample of gunpowder, and a powder flask. If cartridges were unavailable, a percussion revolver like the Tranter could be loaded with powder from the flask and a loose bullet. Powder flasks became obsolete when self-contained cartridges arrived.

Adjustable measuring spout

Metal powder flask

Cartridge cover

Gunpowder

Pistols

A PISTOL IS SIMPLY a short-barreled firearm designed to be used with one hand - a convenient weapon to carry but needing much practice to fire accurately. During the 19th century a great number of pistols were designed for both military and civilian use. Some could fire only a single shot but others - called revolvers - could fire several shots in a row before they needed reloading.

OPEN CYLINDER
The open cylinder of a Colt revolver, shown at the moment when the empty cartridge cases are ejected, before reloading .

One of three bands for holding barrel in stock

COSSACK PISTOL
A pistol from the Caucasus in southern Russia with a miquelet lock - a type of flintlock used mainly in Spain and the Middle East. Cossack warriors used similar pistols in the 18th and 19th century.

"BUNTLINE SPECIAL" REVOLVER *above*
This long-barreled version of the Colt Peacemaker (p. 61) was made famous by the 19th-century American writer Ned Buntline, author of over 400 action novels.

Hammer

ASSASSIN'S PISTOL *below*
This unusual revolver, known as a palm pistol or "lemon squeezer," was held almost hidden in the hand and fired by a squeezing action. One was used to assassinate President William McKinley in 1901.

7-shot cylinder

Barrel

Hammer

TRANSITIONAL REVOLVER *above*
Representing the "transition" between the pepperbox and the true revolver, this weapon was cheap and popular during the 1850s.

Six barrels

Trigger rotates the barrel and fires the shot

PEPPERBOX REVOLVER
The pepperbox was an early form of revolver, with a cluster of barrels, the muzzles of which resembled holes in a pepperpot. Pepperboxes were popular between 1830 and 1860, despite their unreliability.

Bullet mold for
combination pistol

*Folding dagger
blade*

Pistol barrel

*Folding pocket-
knife blade*

*Folding
trigger*

COMBINATION PISTOL

A popular weapon of the 1840s and
'50s was the combined pistol and
pocketknife. This example
includes a pistol, two knife
blades, a ramrod, and
space in the grip for
ammunition.

*Hollow grip
for ammunition and
bullet mold*

*Decorative gilt
and Niello work*

Special 12 in (305 mm) barrel

Ramrod

POCKET OR MUFF PISTOL

This percussion pistol, c. 1850, was kept in a
man's pocket or a lady's muff. Its trigger
folded into the pistol when not in use.

*A .36 caliber
cartridge for the
Colt Police Revolver*

COLT POLICE
REVOLVER *above*

Among the many types of pistol
produced by Colt from the 1830s
onwards was the Model l862 Police
Revolver, a gun firing five shots.

*Lanyard ring for
cord attaching
pistol around
the neck or
shoulder*

*Ejector rod to
knock out empty
cartridge cases*

PINFIRE CARTRIDGE

The pistol's hammer
struck the brass pin,
which set off a detonator
inside the cartridge.

Two barrels

FRENCH PINFIRE REVOLVER

Pinfire weapons were among the
first to use a self-contained cartridge
in which bullet, powder, and cap
were all held in a brass case. The
cartridge could be loaded quickly
from the breech end, and its case
kept the explosion from leaking
back toward the firer's hand. This
revolver dates from about 1855.

"OVER-AND-UNDER" PISTOL

This English pocket pistol,
c. 1820, has two barrels, one above the
other. Each has its own flintlock
mechanism, but a clever design
allows both barrels to be fired by
just one trigger.

Single trigger

Guns that won the West

THE WESTWARD EXPANSION of the United States in the 19th century coincided with a period of rapid development in firearms, and the new arms were used alike by settlers, cowboys, the army, Indians, and outlaws. The most popular weapons were revolvers such as those made by Samuel Colt, and repeating rifles such as the Winchester, which were light enough for use as a carbine on horseback and more accurate than a revolver at longer ranges on the open plains.

Buffalo Bill, holding a Winchester '73, with the Sioux chief Sitting Bull

Iron butt plate

Lever

Lever incorporated with trigger guard pushed forward and back between shots

Spare cartridge

Walnut stock

Belt loop

GUNBELT AND HOLSTER
This much-used 19th-century gunbelt and holster is similar to the one worn by the US cavalry officer in campaign dress (inset), drawn by artist Frederic Remington (1861-1909). Note the spare cartridges in the belt loops.

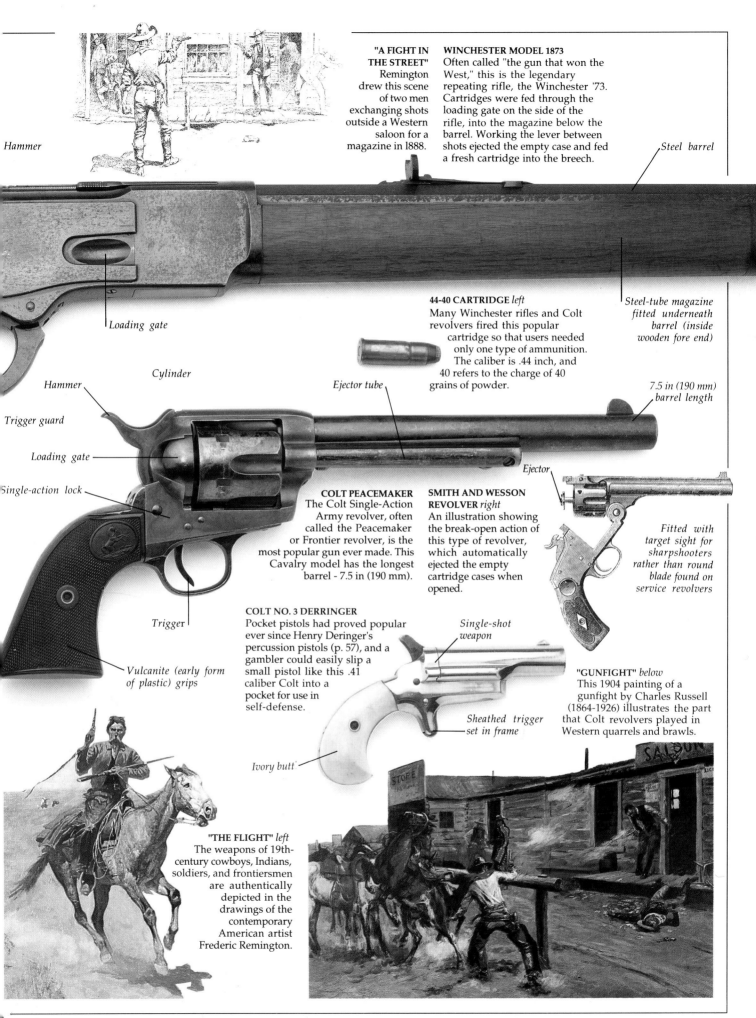

Hammer

"A FIGHT IN THE STREET"
Remington drew this scene of two men exchanging shots outside a Western saloon for a magazine in 1888.

WINCHESTER MODEL 1873
Often called "the gun that won the West," this is the legendary repeating rifle, the Winchester '73. Cartridges were fed through the loading gate on the side of the rifle, into the magazine below the barrel. Working the lever between shots ejected the empty case and fed a fresh cartridge into the breech.

Steel barrel

Loading gate

44-40 CARTRIDGE *left*
Many Winchester rifles and Colt revolvers fired this popular cartridge so that users needed only one type of ammunition. The caliber is .44 inch, and 40 refers to the charge of 40 grains of powder.

Steel-tube magazine fitted underneath barrel (inside wooden fore end)

Cylinder

Hammer

Ejector tube

7.5 in (190 mm) barrel length

Trigger guard

Loading gate

Single-action lock

COLT PEACEMAKER
The Colt Single-Action Army revolver, often called the Peacemaker or Frontier revolver, is the most popular gun ever made. This Cavalry model has the longest barrel - 7.5 in (190 mm).

SMITH AND WESSON REVOLVER *right*
An illustration showing the break-open action of this type of revolver, which automatically ejected the empty cartridge cases when opened.

Ejector

Fitted with target sight for sharpshooters rather than round blade found on service revolvers

Trigger

COLT NO. 3 DERRINGER
Pocket pistols had proved popular ever since Henry Deringer's percussion pistols (p. 57), and a gambler could easily slip a small pistol like this .41 caliber Colt into a pocket for use in self-defense.

Single-shot weapon

Vulcanite (early form of plastic) grips

Sheathed trigger set in frame

"GUNFIGHT" *below*
This 1904 painting of a gunfight by Charles Russell (1864-1926) illustrates the part that Colt revolvers played in Western quarrels and brawls.

Ivory butt

"THE FLIGHT" *left*
The weapons of 19th-century cowboys, Indians, soldiers, and frontiersmen are authentically depicted in the drawings of the contemporary American artist Frederic Remington.

North American Indians

WRONGLY CALLED *Indios* by Christopher Columbus, the native inhabitants of North America once totaled between one and two million people. However, between 1492 and 1900 the Indian tribes were nearly wiped out, as European settlers forced their own way of life on the woodlands and prairies. After initial peaceful contacts with white traders, the tribes who fought hardest to prevent the white man's takeover of their lands in the 1800s were those who lived on the Great Plains and in the Southwest. The Plains Indians lived in the central grasslands, where the more nomadic (roaming) tribes among them hunted the herds of buffalo that crossed the prairies. Other Indian tribes such as the Apaches, fierce warriors from the Southwest, tended to live in one place. Before they obtained European rifles, the tribes in both these areas used basically the same weapons - bows and arrows (p. 9), knives (pp. 22-23), clubs, and the weapon most strongly associated with the North American Indian, the tomahawk.

A typical mask worn by Indians during religious ceremonies

STONE-BLADED KNIFE
All Indians owned knives. This one was made in 1900 by a Hupa Indian from California. By 1900, many Indians had steel-bladed knives.

Finely honed stone blade

HIAWATHA
An Ojibwa Indian, Hiawatha was the hero of a long narrative poem written in 1855 by Henry Longfellow. In it, Hiawatha becomes leader of his people and teaches peace with the white man.

Feather decoration

Cloth strips bound with buckskin

Quiver made of buckskin

Bow made of ash

WAR BOW, c. 1850
Until they began to acquire firearms in the 1850s and 60s, Plains Indians' bows were their most important weapons, used for both hunting and warfare. Made of ash, this bow belonged to an Omaha warrior.

Nock or groove for attachment of bowstring

QUIVER

BOW CASE AND QUIVER
For easier carrying on horseback, a Plains Indian had a combined quiver and bow case. Bow accessories were usually made of buckskin.

BOW CASE

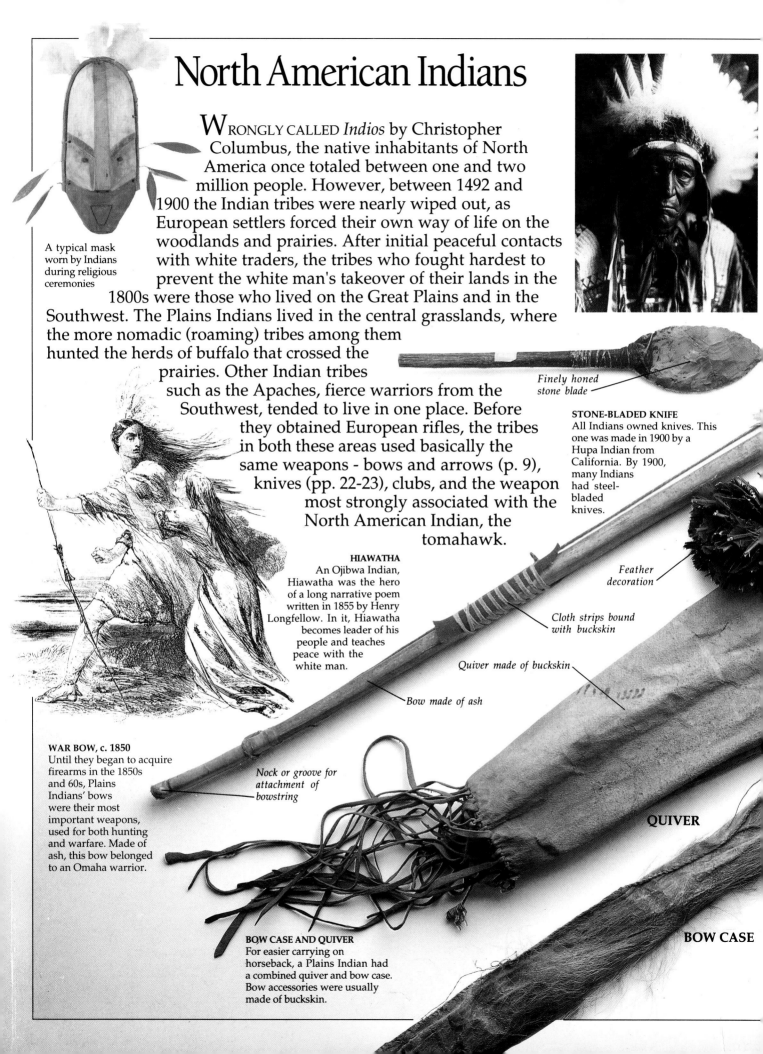

BUFFALO HUNTING
Painter George Catlin spent six years among the Plains Indians, recording their way of life in the early 1800s. In this painting, Indians are hunting buffalo.

TOMAHAWK PIPE, c. 1890
This tomahawk pipe was supposedly made by the great Apache chief Geronimo during his exile in Florida.

Tomahawk blade

EAGLE FEATHER HEADDRESS *left*
In this 1907 photograph, the eagle feather headdress, worn by Iron Plume, a Plains Indian chieftain, was seen only at ceremonies and celebrations.

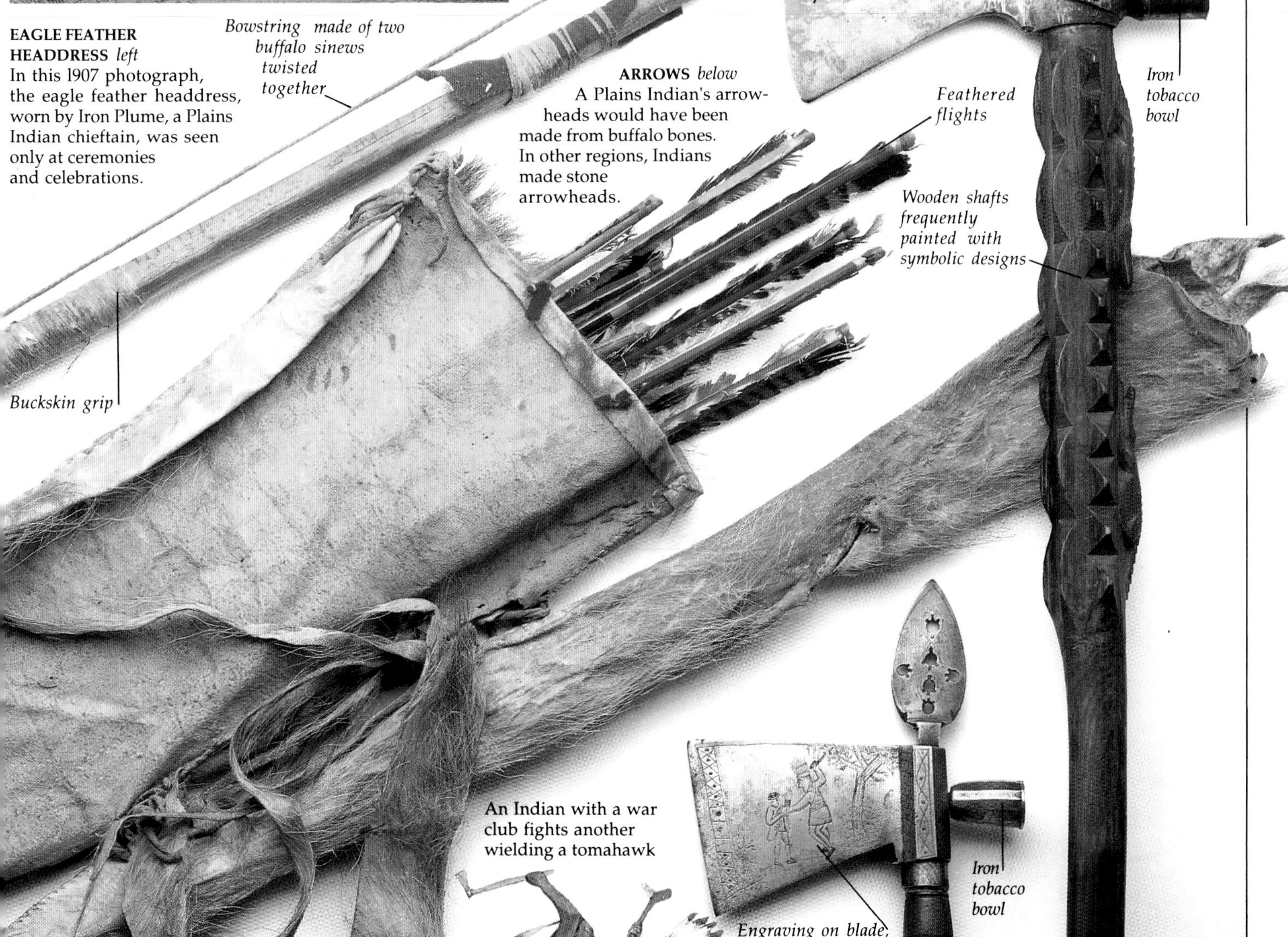

Bowstring made of two buffalo sinews twisted together

ARROWS *below*
A Plains Indian's arrow-heads would have been made from buffalo bones. In other regions, Indians made stone arrowheads.

Feathered flights

Wooden shafts frequently painted with symbolic designs

Iron tobacco bowl

Buckskin grip

An Indian with a war club fights another wielding a tomahawk

Engraving on blade, c. 1800, shows Indian threatening a European

Iron tobacco bowl

Hollow handle

APACHE TOMAHAWK PIPE
Before European traders supplied the Indians with iron, they made their tomahawk heads with stone. The type of tomahawk that combined an axe blade with a tobacco bowl was usually made by Europeans for trading with the Indians.

Did you know?

AMAZING FACTS

Despite modern pictures that show Vikings armed with swords, swords were rare. The most common weapon of the Viking warrior was a long spear, and professional fighters and chieftains usually fought with huge broad-bladed battle axes.

Wooden haft attached here

Viking axe head

Mongol warriors from central Asia were skilled horsemen, and could ride up to 75 miles (120 km) a day and hit a target with a bow and arrow at full gallop.

Mongol archers had whistling arrows for signaling, armor-piercing arrows, and even arrows tipped with a kind of explosive grenade, making them the first warriors to use gunpowder as a weapon.

At one of the largest medieval tournaments ever staged, at Lagny-sur-Marne in France in 1180, more than 3,000 armed and mounted knights fought each other for sport and honor "with no holds barred."

Some jousts were carried out on water. Two teams of rowers propelled their boats toward one another while a knight in each boat's prow tried to knock his opponent off balance with a lance. The English longbow, with its range,

accuracy, and deadly power, was one of the most decisive weapons of the Middle Ages and responsible for the defeat of the French army at Agincourt in 1415, even though English troops were outnumbered by French five to one.

In 1982, 138 preserved longbows were discovered during the excavation of the shipwreck the *Mary Rose*, and historians discovered that a longbow's draw power was twice that supposed.

It took years of training and strength to use a longbow effectively, so longbow practice was compulsory by law in England for men of fighting age so that they maintained their skills.

If caught, the French would cut two fingers off the right and left hand of a longbowman so he couldn't draw his bow.

Because crossbows were slow to load, crossbowmen sometimes worked in pairs, with one reloading behind a shield (called a pavise) while the other fired.

One of the first soldiers to die in battle from wounds inflicted by a cannon ball was an English soldier at Agincourt, in 1415. However, the invention of firearms did not change war all at once. A mixture of swords and pikes alongside muskets and cannon was used in battle throughout the 16th and 17th centuries.

A common weapon among European peasants for hundreds of years was a primitive mace called a Morning Star or Holy Water Sprinkler. This fearsome weapon had a large head, made of iron or wood and studded with spikes, affixed to a long shaft.

Armor was often blued by controlled heating or left black because it was thought to make it less susceptible to rust.

The groove in a sword blade is sometimes wrongly known as a "blood gutter." The groove, or fuller, lightens the blade.

In the 1500s, Queen Elizabeth I of England ordered that gallants' rapiers (which had become dangerously long) be broken if they exceeded 3 ft (1 m).

Some early matchlock muskets were so heavy they had to be fired from a rest and so, effectively, were like small cannons. At the time, cannons were often given the names of animals or birds. "Musket" was the name used by falconers for the male sparrow hawk—the smallest hawk.

Some sword-fighters carried a special weapon in their left hand. This had a serrated edge designed to catch the opponent's rapier blade, which could then be broken with a twist of the wrist.

Mongol archers

After the invention of the wheel-lock, it was possible to make small, easily concealed pistols. Pistols were fitted into the hilt of swords, onto clubs, spears, and crossbows, and even in the handles of knives and forks. Pistols were also combined with other weapons, such as a daggers and knuckledusters.

Breastplate left black from the forging process

Crossbows and longbows at the Battle of Crecy (1346)

QUESTIONS AND ANSWERS

Knight in plate battle armor

Horse armor of the Fulani people of West Africa was made of cotton stuffed with kapok.

Q Could a knight in plate armor get up if he fell down on the battlefield?

A A full suit of plate armor weighed around 44–55 lbs (20–25 kg). However, its weight was spread over the body, so a fit man could run, lie down, get up, and mount a horse unaided. Stories of cranes being used to winch a knight into his saddle are therefore untrue. The secret of a knight's mobility was in the way in which armorers made the plates, which were hinged so that they could move with each other and with the wearer.

Q Did children wear armor?

A In Europe, although a boy of noble birth usually started his training to become a knight from the age of seven, he would not have the money for good-quality armor until he had served his apprenticeship as a squire and had become a knight. This usually happened around the age of 21. However, some rich families did give their young sons gifts of armor. In Japan, ceremonial swords were often given to children when they first put on grown-up or ceremonial clothes.

Q Did animals wear armor?

A In battles during the Middle Ages, knights sometimes covered their horses' heads and flanks with mail to protect them as they fought. Plate horse armor was expensive, so usually, if a knight could only afford part of it, he chose the shaffron—the piece for the head. Similarly, hunting dogs were usually protected against injury from the tusks of wild boars or stag antlers in quilted, padded vests or, occasionally, in plate and mail. Animal armor was also used in countries outside Europe. For example, in India, elephants used in battle were often fitted with protective head and body armor.

Q Do people wear armor today?

A Yes, but although some soldiers wear shiny metal breastplates and carry swords or spears on parade, on the battlefield they wear a type of flak jacket or bulletproof vest and carry guns. Riot police also wear a kind of flak jacket and a protective steel or plastic helmet with a shatterproof visor. Flak jackets are fitted with metal, plastic, or ceramic materials designed to withstand the impact of most types of handgun and some rifle bullets, so the wearer is bruised rather than seriously injured or killed.

Armored elephant

French policeman in riot gear

Q What was the first European firearm?

A No one knows for sure. However, a manuscript written in England in 1326 called the *Milemete Manuscript* shows an illustration of a knight igniting a powder charge in a small cannon shaped like a vase.

Q How were lead bullets made?

A In the 18th century, the lead ball or bullet used in flint-lock dueling pistols was made at home, using a special mold. Molten lead was poured into the mold, which was then opened like a pair of scissors when cooled. Excess lead was trimmed off with scissors.

Record Breakers

FIRST BOW AND ARROW
We know from cave paintings that bows and arrows were made and used in the Sahara region of northern Africa from around 30,000 BCE

LONGEST BOW
The powerful English longbow used from the 13th to 16th centuries was usually as tall as its user. With it, an archer could shoot an arrow up to 1,000 ft (300 m). Some Japanese war bows made of a combination of bamboo and other wood were even longer.

FIRST SWORD
The earliest swords were made in about 1500 BCE, when bronze-working first developed.

LONGEST SWORD
Two-hand swords (large versions of the ordinary sword, swung in both hands) became popular in the 13th century. Some specimens in museums are nearly 6 ft (2m) long.

INVENTION OF GUNPOWDER
The first known recipe for gunpowder was published in 1044 by Chinese chemist Wu Ching Tsao Yao and used in fireworks.

LARGEST GUN
The early musket was the largest gun carried and fired by a single man—some early ones were said to be around 4 ft (1.2 m) long and have a 1 in (2.5 cm) bore.

Bronze sword

Who's who?

WE KNOW LITTLE ABOUT THE SKILLED CRAFTSMEN who made early arms and armor, and some famous swordmakers, such as Masamune, rarely signed their work. Later, however, names were engraved on pieces or they were stamped as a sign of workmanship and quality.

ARMORERS AND SWORDMAKERS

Tsuba

MIOCHIN SCHOOL (1100–c. 1750)
School of Japanese armorers founded in the 12th century by Munesake, famous for its armor and tsuba. Later generations certified work by the school's predecessors that had previously been unsigned.

MASAMUNE (c. 1265–1358)
Famous Japanese swordmaker of Kamakura who rarely signed or decorated his sword blades, believing (as did many Japanese swordsmiths) that a fine-quality blade spoke for itself and did not need the maker's mark to prove its worth.

MISSAGLIA FAMILY (FROM c. 1390)
Family of armorers working in Milan, Italy, which later assumed the family name of Negroni; became famous for highly decorated, elaborate armor.

SEUSENHOFFER BROTHERS (c. 1459–1519)
Court armorers to Emperor Maximilian I. Conrad Seusenhoffer developed the style of fluted armor known as Maximilian armor.

HANS GRUNEWALT (LATE 1400s)
Nuremberg armorer who worked for Emperor Maximilian I.

COLOMAN OR COLMAN (1476–1522)
Augsburg armorer who produced armor for Emperors Maximilian I and Charles V.

TREYTZ FAMILY (c. 1460–1517)
Family of armorers working in Innsbruck, Austria.

NOBUIYE (1485–1564)
Japanese maker of tsuba and armor.

HOPFER BROTHERS (EARLY 1500s)
Augsburg engravers who decorated much of the armor made by Coloman.

JACOB TOPF (1530–97)
Innsbruck armorer who worked for a time at Greenwich, England.

ANDREA FERRARA (1550–1583)
Italian swordsmith whose blades became popular in Scotland; the famed Highland broadswords are often named after him. Another Italian swordmaker, Giandonato, may have been his brother.

JACOBE HALDER (1578–1610)
Master armorer at Greenwich Armoury, England.

ASSAD ULLAH (c. 1588–1628)
Persian swordsmith whose blades were made of finely watered steel.

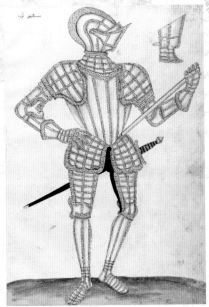
Armor design by Jacobe Halder

GUNMAKERS

HENRY DERRINGER (1786–1868)
American arms maker famous for his distinctive small percussion pistol.

NIKOLAUS VON DREYSE (1787–1867)
German gunsmith who designed a rifle in which bullets were loaded near the trigger, so troops could shoot lying down, safer from enemy fire.

Samuel Colt

SAMUEL COLT (1814–82)
American inventor who took out his first patent for a revolver in 1836; maker of several famous models, such as the Colt .45 and the Colt Peacemaker, which is still in use today.

OLIVER WINCHESTER
Former shirt manufacturer with an interest in firearms who founded the Winchester Repeating Arms Company of Connecticut in 1866.

PHILO REMINGTON (1816–89)
American inventor and the son of the inventor Eliphalet Remington, who ran a small arms factory. Philo managed the factory's mechanical department and became president in 1860; perfected the Remington breech-loading rifle.

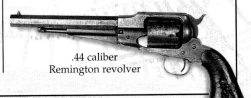
.44 caliber
Remington revolver

RULERS, SOLDIERS, AND HEROES

JULIUS CAESAR (C. 100–44 BCE)
Roman general and statesman whose military campaigns extended Roman power in western Europe. Caesar invaded Britain in 54 and 55 BCE, and also defeated the Gauls.

Alexander the Great

ALEXANDER THE GREAT (356–323 BCE)
Son of Philip II of Macedon and tutored by Aristotle, Alexander ascended the throne as King of Macedonia when he was less than 20 years old. During his reign, he conquered Persia, took control of Egypt, and founded the city of Alexandria.

KING ARTHUR (C. SIXTH CENTURY)
Legendary king of the Britains represented as a unifier of the British tribes and champion of Christianity, who is said to have wielded the mythical sword, *Excalibur*.

CHARLEMAGNE (742–814)
King of the Franks who defeated the Saxons, fought the Arabs in Spain, and took control of most of western Europe. He was crowned Holy Roman Emperor in 800 by the Pope.

Charlemagne

ALFRED THE GREAT (849–99)
King of Wessex, England, who won back land from the Danes, organizing his forces into a standing army and establishing a network of burhs, or fortified centers, which enabled his successors to secure the unity of England.

WILLIAM I, "THE CONQUEROR" (c. 1028–87)
Duke of Normandy and the first Norman King of England who defeated and killed the English king Harold II at the Battle of Hastings in 1066 and replaced Anglo-Saxon leaders with a new ruling class of Normans.

ROBIN HOOD (c. 1250–c.1350)
Legendary English outlaw and hero, said to be unrivaled with a bow and quarter-staff, who lived in Sherwood Forest with his band of "Merry Men," said to rob from the rich and give to the poor.

WILLIAM TELL (c. 1300s)
Legendary Swiss patriot and famous marksman; his killing of the local Austrian steward who had forced him to shoot an apple from his son's head is said to have initiated the movement that secured Switzerland's independence from Austria.

EDWARD, "THE BLACK PRINCE" (1330–76)
Son of Edward III and a great soldier; who fought at the Battle of Crecy (1346) when still a teenager; he is thought to have gained his popular title from his black surcoat, worn when jousting.

HENRY V (1387–1422)
King of England who invaded France in 1415 and won the Battle of Agincourt against great odds, mainly owing to the skill of his longbowmen.

MAXIMILIAN I (1459–1519)
Hapsburg ruler who became Holy Roman Emperor in 1493. His aggressive foreign policy brought him into conflict with the French, Swiss, and Germans. A style of armor with ridges to imitate pleated clothes worn at the time is named after him, although he does not appear to have been connected with it.

HENRY III (1551–89)
King of France from 1574–89, whose reign was marked by civil war between the Huguenots and Catholics; the last of the French Valois kings.

NAPOLEON BONAPARTE (1769–1821)
French artillery officer who became Emperor of France in 1804. Defeated by the British navy at Trafalgar (1805), but dominated Europe after a series of victories on land; forced to abdicate when France was invaded, he regained power but was finally defeated at Waterloo (1815).

DUKE OF WELLINGTON (1769–1852)
British general who was made a duke after his victories against France during the Peninsular War. Along with Prussian forces led by Blücher, defeated the French at the Battle of Waterloo in 1815.

Napoleon

GEBBARD LEBERECHT VON BLÜCHER (1742–1819)
Prussian field marshal who defeated Napoleon Bonaparte at the Battle of Leipzig (1814) then again at Waterloo (1815); known as "Marshal Forward" because his victories were mainly due to the energy and dash of his troops.

JAMES BOWIE (1790–1836)
American pioneer born in Kentucky and the inventor of the dagger, or sheath-knife, named after him. Settled in Texas and became a colonel in the Texan army; killed at the battle of the Alamo in 1836.

WILLIAM FREDERICK CODY (1846–1917)
American army scout and pony express rider; earned the nickname "Buffalo Bill" after killing 5,000 buffalo as part of a contract to supply railroad workers with meat.

Maximilian armor

Find out more

Bᴇᴄᴀᴜsᴇ ᴍᴏsᴛ ᴀʀᴍᴏʀ ᴀɴᴅ ᴡᴇᴀᴘᴏɴʀʏ is made of metal, much has survived through the years. It is possible to see suits of armor, swords, maces, and other weapons in various museums around the world. Many reenactment groups also put on displays to show what warfare was like hundreds of years ago, with members wearing realistic armor and carrying replica arms.

You can often see armor and weaponry from earlier periods in history at state ceremonies or on ceremonial occasions, such as that worn by the Swiss Guards at the Vatican City in Rome (pictured below left).

SEE A MOVIE
Some movies, such *Gladiator* (above) or *Braveheart* show fairly realistic weaponry and armor from different periods. Props for these films are made by armorers, and it is possible to visit their workshops on the Internet.

Walnut stock inlaid with engraved staghorn

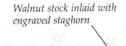

MUSEUM COLLECTIONS
Many national museums contain impressive displays of arms and armor. For example, the Metropolitan Museum of Art in New York has around 15,000 objects in its collection of arms and armor, including examples from Japan, the Middle East, India, and China. The Musée de l'Armée in Paris contains France's national armor collection and includes many pieces from the 16th century and the Napoleonic era. Some private collections are also open to the public, such as the Wallace Collection in London. It is also possible to see armor on display at castles or stately homes.

ARMORIES
Some of the world's great armories—in Vienna, Madrid, Paris, Dresden, and London—have extensive collections where you can see a range of body armor and weapons. The display pictured above shows arms and armor from the 15th to 17th centuries, which is housed in the War Gallery at the Royal Armouries Museum in Leeds, England.

DEMONSTRATIONS

The Royal Armouries at the Tower of London sometimes gives members of the public the opportunity to handle both original and replica objects. Many armories also put on demonstrations. For example, the Royal Armouries Museum in Leeds has a Craft Court where it is possible to see armorers, a leather-worker, and gunmakers at work using traditional techniques. These craftworkers make many of the replicas used in the museum during hands-on demonstrations. The museum also has a Tiltyard where performers put on exhibitions of military and sporting skills, such as jousts.

Clothing made by leather-workers at Leeds Armoury, such as the 17th-century-style buffcoat (left), is worn by staff members.

FIREARMS

Many national museums have collections of firearms. This wheel-lock, breech-loading pistol, on display at the Victoria and Albert Museum in London, was made by Hans Stockman in Dresden, Germany, c. 1600.

USEFUL WEB SITES

- For information about museum exhibits and traveling collections of arms and armor:
  www.aas-usa.net
- The Musée de l'Armée virtual gallery of arms from the medieval period to World War II:
  www.invalides.org/invalidesgb/indexgb/pagesgb/accueilcolecgb.html
- For information and photographs of swords of different cultures and time periods:
  swordforum.com
- For a virtual tour of the collections at the Met:
  www.metmuseum.org/collections/

REENACTMENT SOCIETIES

Many different groups in the United States, such as the Napoleonic Society, pictured below, and others around the world reenact scenes or battles from various periods in history., Other societies stage medieval combat or battles from the English Civil War. Find out if any are staging an event near you through the Web site listed in the box on the left.

Places to visit

THE METROPOLITAN MUSEUM OF ART, NEW YORK, NEW YORK

The Museum's internationally recognized Department of Arms and Armor includes arms and armor from ancient Egypt, classical Greece and Rome, Japan, and Europe. Special galleries are devoted to American arms from the colonial-era and the late 19th-century, and arms from Islamic cultures, including a series of decorated armor from Iran and Anatolia and jewel-studded weapons from the Ottoman Turkish and Mughal Indian courts.

FRAZIER HISTORICAL ARMS MUSEUM, LOUISVILLE, KENTUCKY

Opened in 2004, this museum houses a unique combination of arms from both the United States and Great Britain. The extensive collection includes weaponry belonging to such important historical figures as Henry VII, Geronimo, and Theodore Roosevelt. There are also two reenactment areas with live demonstrations.

CLEVELAND MUSEUM OF ART, CLEVELAND, OHIO

The museum's collection focuses on medieval armor and weaponry, including swords, crossbows, and daggers. There are also several 16th and 17th century firearms from throughout Europe.

DEWITT WALLACE DECORATIVE ARTS MUSEUM, COLONIAL WILLIAMSBURG, VIRGINIA

The museum holds an extensive collection of military and civilian firearms from the Revolutionary War period. Williamsburg itself is a living museum with a gunsmith shop and the Governor's Palace, with its main hall decorated in arms.

HIGGINS ARMORY MUSEUM, WORCESTER, MASSACHUSSETS

This museum has five floors displaying over 8,000 pieces of armor and weaponry. Different galleries are devoted to the tournament, hunting, ancient arms, and armor, the armorer's craft and arms and armor from around the world. There is also a combat wing.

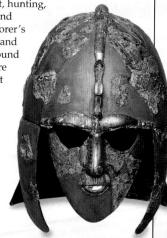

Helmet found at Sutton Hoo, on display at the British Museum in London, England

Glossary

Artilleryman

ARMORER A metal-worker specializing in making armor; in Europe the craft of the armorer was regulated by a guild.

ARQUEBUS Originally, a kind of heavy matchlock gun; later, the word was used to mean a wheel-lock gun and, finally, a gun of fine workmanship rather than a common musket

ARTILLERY Originally, "artillery" meant any machine used to throw stones and other missiles; later it was used for cannon

BASCINET Helmet popular during the 14th century, some with a plate visor to protect the face (*see also* VISOR)

BAYONET Blade designed to fit into or over a gun muzzle

BLUNDERBUSS Short gun or pistol with a large bore and wide muzzle that fired a number of small shots.

BOLT Short, heavy arrow used with the crossbow; a bolt with a four-sided head was sometimes known as a quarrel (*see also* CROSSBOW)

BREECH-LOADER Firearm loaded from the breech or back part of a gun, rather than the muzzle at the front

Burgonet

BROADSWORD Heavy military sword with a wide, straight blade

BURGONET Helmet originating in Burgundy, worn by cavalrymen and infantry officers in the 16th century

CAVALRY Mounted soldiers, often divided into two main groups—light cavalry (whose main tasks were scouting and pursuit of a beaten enemy), and heavy cavalry (used for shock impact: that is, charging in solid lines).

CLAYMORE Double-edged, two-hand broadsword with a long, heavy blade, used by Scottish Highlanders in the 15th and 16th centuries; means "great sword" from the Gaelic *claidheamhmhor*

COIF Mail hood worn under a helmet

CROSSBOW Popular weapon in medieval Europe, in which a cord was drawn back to shoot arrows called bolts or quarrels. Most crossbows were so powerful that mechanical means were needed to span or draw them.

CUIRASS Type of body armor comprising a breastplate and backplate worn together and usually fastened by straps or buckles; originally made of leather, then later of bronze, then steel

DUELING PISTOL High-quality, muzzle-loading pistol, usually supplied in a box as a pair, with accessories for making bullets, cleaning, and loading

DUELING SWORD Sword developed for dueling after people stopped carrying swords as part of daily life

FENCING The art and skill of fighting with a rapier; developed in France and Italy in the early 17th century

FLAIL Weapon in which an iron or wooden ball sometimes studded with spikes was attached to a haft, or handle, by a chain, or to a bar by a swivel. (*see also* MACE)

FLINTLOCK Type of gun invented in the late 1500s in which flint is struck against a steel hammer, sending sparks into the priming powder and igniting the main charge. Its lock had to be set to "full cock" before firing, making it safer to use.

FULLER Groove down the length of the sword to lighten the blade

GAUNTLET Hand armor

GLADIUS Short, double-edged thrusting sword used by Roman infantry

GREAVE European armor for the lower leg, at first just for the shin but later also including a part to protect the calf

GRENADIERS Originally, troops trained to use hand-grenades; grenadiers wore low caps which made it easier for them to sling a musket over their shoulder, leaving both hands free to light and throw a grenade. By the 19th century, the word grenadier was used for ordinary infantry troops.

Dagger

GUILD A medieval association that controlled and regulated a particular craft, such as armor-making (*see also* PROOF)

HALBERD Kind of staff weapon made up of a long wooden handle mounted with an axe blade, backed by a hook, and topped by a spike

HAND-GRENADE Hollow iron ball filled with explosive and threaded with a short fuse. The first hand-grenades came into use in the 17th century. (*see also* GRENADIERS)

Mempo

HARAMAKI Japanese cuirass worn by foot soldiers comprising a breastplate and skirts (called *kasazuri*) to protect the lower body

HARNESS Full suit of armor

HAUBERK Long tunic made of mail

HELM Helmet that completely enclosed the head and face, usually cylindrical, used from the early 1200s

HILT End of a sword made up of a grip to hold it, a pommel for balance, and (sometimes) a protective hand guard

INFANTRY Foot soldiers

JOUST Contest in a tournament in which two charging knights tried to dismount each other with lances (*see also* TOURNAMENT)

KABUTO Japanese helmet

KATANA Long fighting sword used by Japanese samurai

KRISS Malysian knife with a range of blade-shapes, hilts, and scabbards

LONGBOW Tall, powerful bow used in Europe in the Middle Ages; usually made from one piece of shaped and honed yew, from the heartwood (which resists compression) and the sapwood (which resists tension), therefore forming a strong, natural spring

MACE Weapon with a haft and a metal head. Some heads were spiked, others were ridged to penetrate armor. (*see also* FLAIL)

MATCHLOCK Gun with an early, simple kind of firing mechanism in which an S-shaped lever was pressed down to force a match into a flashpan, which ignited the powder; later replaced by the flintlock

MAXIMILIAN ARMOR Name given to a style of 16th century plate armor with narrow fluting popular during the reign of Holy Roman Emperor, Maximilian I

MEMPO Japanese face armor, some of which was decorated to resemble old men, demons, or ghosts

MORION HELMET Type of lightweight, open helmet often made of a single piece of steel with a broad brim and peak and cheekpieces; popular in the mid-16th century and worn mainly by infantry.

MUSKET Originally used to mean a matchlock gun which was fired from a rest (because of its weight). Later, the name came to mean any gun used by infantry.

MUSKETEER Infantry soldier armed with a musket

PAULDRON Piece of European plate armor covering the shoulder

PAVISE Large wooden shield used to protect archers and crossbowmen when loading and firing their weapons

Guild marks from Umbria, Italy

PERCUSSION LOCK Form of ignition for both muzzle- and breech-loading firearms, introduced in the early 1800s, in which a hammer hits a detonating mixture that explodes and fires the bullet

PIKEMAN Infantry soldier usually armed with a pike, or long spear, sword, and buckler (shield), and, in the 17th century, protected from musket fire by a morion helmet and cuirass

POMMEL Rounded weight on the hilt of a sword to balance the sword blade; from the French word "*pomme*," meaning apple

PROOF To test armor by firing a crossbow bolt at it from short range and later a musket; proofed pieces were sometimes stamped with the maker's or guild's mark.

RAPIER Sword with a sharp point, usually with a complex hilt covering the hand and bars protecting the knuckles

SABATON Foot armor covering the upper side of the foot and secured by straps and/or laces

SHAFFRON Armor for a horse's head

SHAMSHIR Lightweight hunting sword originating in Persia; later called a scimitar

SMALLSWORD Light form of the rapier, with a triangular blade designed for thrusting; used from the late 1600s until the late 1700s when they were known as "town" or "walking" swords because they were mostly used as fashion acccessories

SPUR Point fitted to the heel of a rider used to speed up a horse; often seen as the badge of knighthood (from the saying "when a knight won his spurs")

STILETTO Small dagger with a slender blade designed for thrusting

TILT Barrier introduced in the 15th century to separate jousting knights

TOURNAMENT Mock fight originally to train men for war; later became a display of fighting skills with complex rules; included the tourney or melée (between two groups that fought on horseback), the joust, and, later, the foot combat

Shaffron

TSUBA Japanese sword guard

TULWAR Curved Indian sword

VAMBRACE European plate armor worn on the arm

VISOR Protective armor for the face, introduced around 1300, which was hinged and could be swung up. Some visors could be detached from the helmet for cleaning or for repair. (*see also* HELMET)

WAKIZASHI Short Japanese sword used as an second fighting sword by a samurai warrior (after the *katana*)

WHEEL-LOCK Gun with a later form of ignition than the matchlock, in which sparks from a spinning wheel were showered into the pan, thereby setting off the charge. The wheel-lock was later replaced by the flintlock. (*see also* FLINTLOCK)

WINDLASS Mechanism with pulleys and handles that fitted over the butt of a crossbow, enabling the crossbow's cord to be wound back tightly, ready for shooting (*see also* CROSSBOW)

Jousting knights

Index

Acknowledgments

The publisher would like to thank:
City of London Police: pp. 54-55; also Police Constable Ray Hayter for his assistance; Pitt Rivers Museum, University of Oxford: pp. 4-5, 22-23, 32-33, 36-37; also John Todd for his assistance; Ermine Street Guard: pp. 1, 12-13; also Nicholas Fuentes for his assistance; Museum of London: pp. 6-7, 10-11, 12bl, 14-15; also Nick Merriman, Peter Stott, and Gavin Morgan for their assistance; Museum of Mankind, British Museum: pp. 8-9, 62-63; National Army Museum: pp. 56-57; also Stephen Bull for his assistance; Warwick Castle, Warwick: pp. 16-17, 24-25, 26-27, 28-29, 30-31, 38-39, 40-41, 42-43, 44-45, 48-49, 52-53, 55t; also F.H.P Barker for his assistance; Robin Wigington, Arbour Antiques, Ltd., Stratford-upon-Avon: pp. 2-3, 18-19, 20-21, 34-35, 38b, 50-51, 58-59, 60-61; also Anne-Marie Bulat for her work on the initial stages of the book; Martyn Foote for design assistance; Fred Ford and Mike Pilley of Radius Graphics, and Ray

Owen and Nick Madren for artwork; Jonathan Buckley for his assistance on the photographic sessions; Coral Mula for the illustration on p6.
The publisher would also like to thank Chris Gravett for his assistance on the revised edition.
The publisher would like to thank the following for their kind permission to reproduce their photographs:
Picture credits:
a=above, b=below, c=center, l=left, r=right, t=top
Lesley and Roy Adkins: 64–65
The Art Archive: 70tl; Bibliotheque Nationale Paris 64bl; British Library: 70-71; Museo dell'Opera del Duomo Orvieto/Dagli Orti 71tc; Oriental Art Museum Genoa/Dagli Orti 66tr.
Reproduced by Courtesy of the Trustees of the British Museum: 14bm.
© The Board of Trustees of the Armouries: 65tl, 68br, 69tr.
Bridgeman Art Library, London / New York: British Library 64cr, 65tl; The Stapleton Collection 71bl; Victoria & Albert Museum

68-69c; Victoria & Albert Museum, London 66cl.
British Museum: 67cr, 69br, 70tr.
Corbis: Ali Meyer 67bl; Araldo de Luca 66-67, 67tl; Michael S. Yamashita 68-69; Philadelphia Museum of Art 70bl; Sygma/Graham Tim 68bl.
Danish National Museum: 64tl.
E.T. Archives: 8b.
English Heritage: Paul Lewis 69b.
Gettysburg National Military Park: 66br.
Giraudon: 43tl.
Goteborg Museum of Art: 39c.
India Office Library (British Library): 33t.
John Freeman London: 16br; 18c, tr; 19cr; 21tr; 26b; 28cr, bl; 30tc; 31t; 39t; 40m; 42b; 44tl; 52t; 53b; 54t; 62tl, tr, c.
H. Josse, Paris: 44b.
Kobal Collection: Dreamworks/Universal/ Buitendijk, Jaap 68tl.
Mansell Collection: 11m; 42c.
Mary Evans Picture Library: 6b; 7bl; 8c; 9b; 12t, br; 13t, b; 14bl; 16bl, t; 17tr, tr; 19t; 20t, c, b; 22t, c; 23c; 24b; 25c, b; 26tl, tr; 27b; 28bc; 29bl, br; 30c, tl, tr; 34tl; 35t; 36c; 38c; b; 39b; 40tl; 44tr; 47tr, b; 48c; 49c; 51c; 52tr, c; 54t, b; 55c; 56t; 57tl, tr; 58tl, tr, b; 60b; 61c, t, 66bl.

Michael Holford: 12bl, 15t, c, b; 32b; 36-37t; 63t.
Museum of London: 65br.
National Army Museum: 53t.
Peter Newark's Western Americana and Historical Pictures: 14br; 29c; 37c; 41b; 46t; 47tl; 56b; 60t; 61br; 63b.
Rex Features: 65bc.
Robert Hunt Library: 21c.
Sheridan Photo Library: 7br.
Tower of London Royal Armouries: 25t.
Visual Arts Library: 43tr, c; 61bl.
The Wallace Collection: 64br, 67br, 71cr.
Jacket images: Front: Ermine Street Guard, UK, b; National Army Museum, London, UK, tl; Warwick Castle, UK, cl; Museum of Mankind, UK, tc; Bettmann/Corbis, tcr Pitt Rivers Museum, Oxford, UK, tr. Back: Pitt Rivers Museum, Oxford, UK, tl; Robin Wigington, Arbour Antiques, cl; Warwick Castle, bl; Museum of London, tr.

All other images © Dorling Kindersley. For further information see: www.dkimages.com